JOSEPH STALIN

JOSEPH
STALIN

by

Janet Caulkins

AN IMPACT

BIOGRAPHY

FRANKLIN WATTS
New York London Toronto Sydney
1990

Diagram and map by Joe LeMonnier
Photographs courtesy of: Sovfoto: pp. 2, 51, 56,
91; Tass/Sovfoto: p. 68; Novosti/Sovfoto: p. 140
(G. Kmit); UPI/Bettmann Newsphotos: pp. 14, 33, 109,
114, 122, 126, 139, 143; The Bettmann Archive: p. 27.

Library of Congress Cataloging-in-Publication Data
Caulkins, Janet.
Joseph Stalin / by Janet Caulkins.
p.   cm. — (An Impact biography)
Includes bibliographical references.
Summary: A biography of the Soviet leader, focusing on his
formative years in Soviet Georgia, his rise to the top of the
Communist party, and his leadership during World War II.
ISBN 0-531-10945-3
1. Stalin, Joseph, 1879–1953—Juvenile literature.   2. Heads of
state—Soviet Union—Biography—Juvenile literature.   3. Soviet
Union—History—1925–1953—Juvenile literature.   [1. Stalin,
Joseph, 1879–1953.   2. Heads of state.   3. Soviet Union—
History—1925–1953.]   I. Title.
DK268.S8C33   1990
947.084′2′092—dc20
[B]   [92]   90-32524 CIP   AC

CONTENTS

INTRODUCTION

As a child he was called "Soso," a pet name for Joseph. In 1917 Joseph Vissarionovich Djugashvili called himself Stalin—a man "made of steel." At the end of World War II, Americans called him "Uncle Joe."

He has been called a brutal monster, a hero with a few faults; a simple man, a complex man; a vain man, a modest one; a genius, a clod; a man with a vision, a man with none; and often, a dangerous psychotic, separated from the real world by suspicions and delusions. He became one of the most powerful and absolute tyrants the world has ever known.

It took Stalin little over a decade to transform Russia from a lumbering, backward, nearly feudal nation of illiterate peasants to one of the foremost industrial and military nations of the world.

Stalin liquidated a hundred thousand farmers in the name of progress, killed half a million intellectuals to eliminate opposition, executed all his top army officers to consolidate his power, and then "purged" his own secret police. He unleashed a famine that starved millions. Then he led Russia to victory over one of the largest armies ever to invade a foreign land.

At the height of his power he stifled art, literature, and all the natural sciences.

How did one man virtually create the great industrial power that we know today? How did he come to exert such a stranglehold on the smallest aspect of the everyday life of its people? At the height of Stalin's power everything—what people ate, what they read, the paintings they looked at, the movies they saw, what they heard on the radio, where they lived, what jobs they held—everything was in one man's control. No control like it has ever existed.

If the familiar words of the philosopher Santayana are true, that "those who cannot remember the past are condemned to repeat it," then it is important for us to examine the life of Joseph Stalin and the events of those years following the Russian Revolution of 1917.

JOSEPH
STALIN

C H A P T E R   1

YOUNG STALIN, OLD RUSSIA

Joseph Stalin was born in the Russia of the czars—
the largest country in the world. This sprawling
giant of a land was unimaginably different from any
of the other great nations of its time. The Russian
Empire held one-tenth of the world's population,
but 90 percent of its people were peasants, living as
if the 1870s were still the Middle Ages. They
dressed in rags and lived in hovels, and "that other
tyrant"—hunger—ruled their day-to-day lives.
Most of what the peasants harvested went to feed
the priests, soldiers, and nobles of the classes above
them.

Serfdom had existed in Russia into the nineteenth century, even though it had long since disappeared from the rest of Europe. A serf in Russia had
been a slave, bound to the nobleman who owned the
land. After serfdom was abolished in 1861, the
peasants had to pay for their so-called freedom with
crushing taxes, exacted by the landlord and the
church—and they were often worse off than before.

The men and women who were to lead the Revolution of 1917 came mostly from educated, well-off families. They were appalled at the plight of the peasants, but many also tended to be romantic and sentimental about the poor—the "honest, sturdy tillers of the soil." Stalin had no such illusions. Desperate poverty did not breed dignity or greatness of soul any more then than now. His own experience as a member of the peasant class was brutalizing and humiliating. Except for Stalin, no leader of a great nation has ever come from such a beginning.

The lot of the factory workers was no better than that of the peasants. In the cities, industry was beginning to grow. Factories in Russia were huge caverns, gathering around them whole populations in smoky, filthy slums. Men and women worked fourteen to sixteen hours a day, seven days a week. The workers had no rights: no civil rights, no "human rights," no legal rights. No laws protected them. They suffered hunger, disease, and early death.

The empire in which these people lived was (and is) a fantastic collection of different nationalities. The empire was named after its original vast core, Great Russia (now the Russian Soviet Federated Socialist Republic). The ruler's title was "Czar of all the Russias." The people of this Russian Empire lived in plains and mountains, in Asian deserts and Arctic snows.

Today Great Russia is still the largest and most important of the Soviet Republics, and even today a native of Moscow will say (often scornfully) of a visitor, "He is not Russian; he is from Georgia," or "She is Ukrainian."

Czar Nicholas II inherited this vast untidy empire. Like the czars before him, he was an absolute ruler, "appointed" by God and anointed by the church. All the ministers of government were hired or fired by him. No laws constrained him, and there was no court through which the people could appeal to him.

It was in this atmosphere that revolutionary groups of all sorts began to grow. One group, the Bolsheviks, seized power in 1917 (eventually murdering the czar and his family). After the Revolution, they renamed themselves the Communist Party. The Communists were led by two men, now famous in history, V. I. Lenin and Leon Trotsky. With them, in the background, was the man Trotsky later called "morally coarse and unscrupulous."[1] That ambitious peasant-class provincial was Joseph Djugashvili, who would become Joseph Stalin, the most powerful ruler in the world.

SOSO DJUGASHVILI

Stalin was born on December 9, 1879. His full name was Joseph Vissarionovich Djugashvili. Like most children in Russia named Joseph, he was called Soso for short. Soso's dangerous and fateful life began in a small town called Gori in Georgia, in the south of the empire, near the Black Sea.

From the very beginning, the dice were loaded against Soso. First of all, his parents were peasants; indeed, his father, Vissarion, had begun life as a serf. (In Georgia, serfdom persisted until the late 1860s.) After serfdom was abolished, Vissarion became a cobbler, making and repairing shoes and boots. He was not a successful cobbler, possibly because he drank heavily. (He was eventually killed in a drunken fight.)

Vissarion seems to have been crude, harsh, and brutal, and he beat his small son often.[2] In later years, Stalin denied this, saying "my parents did not treat me badly," but by then Stalin was busy

"Soso" Djugashvili, age fourteen.

rewriting history to suit himself. His daughter, Svetlana, remembers Stalin's telling her of his childhood, his drunken father, and the violence of his family life. And there were others, among them Stalin's childhood companion Joseph Iremashvili, to confirm it. Iremashvili, who had been his playmate and friend from the age of four or five, always felt that the beatings young Joseph suffered gave him a hatred of authority. Iremashvili said that anyone who had power over other people reminded Joseph of his father. (Iremashvili, we might add, was one of the very few among Stalin's old comrades who survived, as Stalin in later years got rid of almost everyone who had "known him when.")

Soso's mother, Ekaterina—Keke for short—was only twenty years old when Soso was born, and she had already borne three children who had died. Keke was deeply religious, strong, and stubborn. Determined that Joseph would survive and get an education that would lift him out of the peasant class, she decided that her son would become a priest. But that was not going to be easy. Georgia was full of old, landed noble families, and Soso was a peasant, the lowest of the low. His identity card actually read "Joseph Djugashvili, peasant." It might as well have read "Joseph Djugashvili, nobody."

Soso was born in a two-room house. One room was the kitchen. The other was the cobbler's shop, family room, and bedroom all in one, with a bunk built into the wall, a large table, and a few chairs. A trickle of waste water ran down the center of the dirt road in front. (Many years later Stalin's chief of security, Lavrenti Beria, had a huge marble and steel monument built around this hovel.)

Poverty and a drunken father were not the only problems for Soso. When he was seven he barely survived smallpox, a deadly and disfiguring disease. It left him with a scarred and pockmarked face for the rest of his life. In fact, the czar's secret police later had a code name for him, "Riaboi," which means "the pockmarked one." Soso had other physical disadvantages as well. According to records of the czar's police, he was born with "webbed" toes on one foot—that is, two of his toes were joined. Besides the webbed toes and the pockmarked face, an accident, which led to blood poisoning, left Joseph with a short, somewhat malformed left arm. But Soso was as tough as a root and had a will of iron like his mother. And these physical disadvantages did have a useful side; they kept him out of the czar's army.

GEORGIA

Apart from his family background, the very place where he grew up helped to mold young Soso Djugashvili into a rebel. Georgia, where Soso lived until he was twenty-seven, had been an independent kingdom only a hundred years before. It was beautiful, mountainous country, between the Black and Caspian seas, with a mild climate, flourishing vineyards, and flocks of grazing sheep. But it was also backward and primitive. In Georgia serfdom had been abolished late—only fifteen years before Joseph Djugashvili was born.

Georgia was home to a mixture of independent peoples. Over the course of 2,000 years it had been invaded, attacked, settled, or visited by Greeks, Romans, Turks, Armenians, Mongols, Slavs, Jews, and Persians. In the mountains lived tribes who still wore medieval armor—horsemen would come down from the hills armed with sword and dagger, and decked out in black and silver.

One of Joseph's heroes was a character of legend—

a rebel called Koba. Koba was a fierce mountain tribesman, a guerrilla fighter for Georgian independence. Koba was one of the many names Joseph took for himself as a young revolutionary, and he relished being called Koba by those close to him long after he had become "The Great Stalin." (In this book you will find him called Soso, Koba, and Stalin.)

Georgia blended the cultures of the West and the Orient. It had its own language with fifteen or more different dialects. Stalin's parents never learned Russian; he himself knew no Russian until he was seven or eight years old, and he always spoke it with a thick Georgian accent that embarrassed him. Even in later years, people who knew Stalin said his character was "oriental," and more than once he characterized himself as oriental or Asiatic.

This Georgia of many cultures, now under the czar of Russia, preserved its own fierce eccentric character. The different ethnic groups, full of mutual dislike and mistrust, competed with one another and conspired for independence. Yet they were united by one thing: hatred of the Russians.

GEORGIA AND THE RUSSIANS

Georgia was of real importance to the czar because of its location. Linking east and west, north and south, it was a protection and buffer on the southern borders of the Russian Empire. The government, therefore, set out to "Russify" Georgia, and Russians poured into the state. There were soldiers and traders, petty government officials, administrators and priests—and teachers. When Soso was ten or eleven all the teachers at the Gori school were fired and replaced by Russian teachers, who mocked the thick Georgian accent and treated their pupils with disdain.

Soso hated being ordered to do anything, and he resented being forced to study in Russian. He learned Russian as required, though, because he was very much aware that schooling was his only chance to gain control of his own life. But he stirred up demonstrations against the Russian teachers, who in turn punished him, adding fuel to his furious resentment of anyone who had power over him.

It is interesting that Stalin began his revolutionary career as a Georgian nationalist, hating the Russians, for he ended up loving Russia and considering himself Russian rather than Georgian. As an adult, he acted as if he despised the emotional and spontaneous nature of the Georgian people, for whom "fools" became his kindest word. In later years, in Moscow with his second wife and his children, he seldom spoke of Georgia or his childhood there. His daughter Svetlana describes the day her brother said to her, "You know, Papa used to be a Georgian." However, those years when he "used to be a Georgian" instilled in Joseph Djugashvili the habit of rebellion and the taste for mastery over others.

AT SCHOOL IN GORI

All we know about Stalin's school days comes from the reminiscences of a few comrades who knew him in those days and from stories he told his daughter when she was small. Some sources say he was good at sports and wrestling, although his lame arm makes that seem unlikely. Admiring accounts of his swimming ability contrast with his daughter's statement that he didn't know how to swim. Whether or not he enjoyed sports, it seems clear he was far from a "good sport." He could not bear to lose; he had to be first at everything, had to be the one in control.

Soso must have learned early that scorn, contempt, and rage could be powerful weapons. He used them to intimidate even his wealthy schoolmates who might otherwise have picked on the uncouth peasant boy in their midst.

Although he didn't like his Russian teachers, Soso had brains and he got good marks. He was never an "intellectual" like Lenin or Trotsky, but he was an outstanding student at the school in Gori. He graduated in the top group in his class, which qualified him to go on to the Tiflis Theological Seminary and earned him a small scholarship.

In Georgia, the only way out of the dismal existence of the lower classes, especially for a non-Russian, was through the Russian Orthodox Church. With a good church-school education a lower-class boy could possibly become a priest—a huge step up the social and economic scale. It was the priesthood that Keke saw as the future for her son; she took in washing to earn the necessary extra money, and sent him off to school in "the big city."

C H A P T E R 2

THE YOUNG REVOLUTIONARY

Soso's childhood experiences in Gori made him defensive and angry and gave him a lack of compassion for others that would mark him all his life. Now he set off for school in Tiflis, the capital of Georgia. At the Theological Seminary in Tiflis he became, in his own words "an apprentice of the Revolution."[1]

Georgia, full of hotheads and rebels, was not the place to allow open universities where new ideas were always arising. The government found it safer to allow only religious schools, run by Russian Orthodox priests. As a result, of course, the hotheads and rebels had to go to the religious schools if they wanted an education. The Tiflis Theological Seminary was full of students who were seething with anger and plotting against the czar.

At the seminary, fourteen-year-old Soso developed an even greater contempt for religion, for authority, and for most of his fellow human beings. The education that was supposed to make him a priest made him an atheist and a lifelong enemy of the church. The priests at the school were bigoted and dogmatic. They taught him intolerance, and kept him ignorant of the world outside of Russia. In the harsh and hypocritical atmosphere at the seminary, he polished the techniques of conspiracy and manipulation that would help him to power but would leave him in old age isolated, afraid of enemies, and even afraid of friends.

At the seminary, students learned church doctrine, Greek, Latin, authorized literature, and Russian history. But seminary education was severely one-sided. No foreign languages or world history was taught. Higher mathematics, science, and art were ignored, and Stalin never grew to understand any of them. Openness, tolerance, respect for other points of view were not in the curriculum.

The day began for these teenage students with a church service that sometimes lasted as long as four hours—and was endured standing up, which is the Orthodox Church custom. Curfew was at 5:00 and the students were allowed outside the stony walls for only a few hours a week.

The seminary was run like a prison. Although there was no corporal punishment, solitary confinement was almost worse. Students were shut up in a cell for days or weeks as the common penalty for disobeying any of the rules. Soso, for example, was given a long sentence for being caught with a novel by Victor Hugo, whose works had far too much social commentary to be acceptable in the seminary.

The classes were taught by contemptuous and overbearing Russian priests. They were hostile teachers and very suspicious of their Georgian students. The "ferocious monk," Abashidze, searched the students' rooms and set the students spying on one another until no one was sure who among his fellows could be trusted. Stalin later said it was this "spying and prying" that made him a revolutionary.[2]

It was a technique that he would make his own as leader of the Soviet Union.

THE FAMOUS BOOK OF KARL MARX

For Soso Djugashvili the road to revolution began with forbidden reading. At that time—toward the end of the nineteenth century—rebellion was in the air all over Europe. Journalists, philosophers, economists, historians, and novelists wrote about social conditions. Strikes and protests kept governments jittery and in a mood for repression. In this atmosphere, the German writer Karl Marx wrote a book that shook the world of his time. It was called *Das Kapital* (*Capital*) and it was about wealth, poverty, and social class. Soso smuggled excerpts from this book into the seminary where he and his friends read them by candlelight.

The oppression of the laboring class outraged Karl Marx. He developed a theory that prophesied a workers' revolution. His book was long, and the theory was complex and difficult, but *Das Kapital* carried a powerful message. Bringing the theory vividly to life, Marx filled his book with detailed descriptions of child labor, misery, disease, injustice, and the horrors of existence in the mines and factories of the nineteenth-century industrial world.

What then was this "Marxist theory" that stirred up so many people like Joseph Djugashvili? In brief, Marx hammered away at two particular points. First: the "haves" got rich on the labor of the "have-nots." That is, the owners of industry (capitalists) got rich on profits that came from the labor of the workers (proletarians). The workers were enslaved and exploited by their bosses.

The workers, Marx said, would be squeezed until

they had no choice but to rebel. Then they would revolt and destroy the capitalists. There would be a "dictatorship of the proletariat." Factories would be owned by the people in common, and they would no longer be run for profit, but just to supply the needs of the people. There would be no private property except what was needed for one's day-to-day life and work.

In the end, social classes would disappear altogether; government itself would wither away. A worldwide classless society would emerge. Everyone would contribute to the community according to his age and talent. Goods would be distributed "from each according to his abilities, to each according to his needs."

The second leg upon which Marxism stood was the idea that world revolution of the working class was scientifically inevitable. It would happen, and there was no way to stop it. It was, said Marx, a "law of history." To the revolutionaries it meant they could not lose. Revolution was destiny.

Marx's inflammatory book was legally distributed in Russia, partly because it was supposed to apply only to industrial nations, and partly because the czar's censor thought no one would read it. But Soso Djugashvili read it and shared its sense of rage and indignation. The most important student of Marx, however, happened to be another Russian, Vladimir Ilyich Lenin. Lenin, nine years older than Stalin, was the man who would lead the Marxist Revolution in Russia and who would set Stalin on the road to power.

CITY OF REVOLUTIONARIES

Tiflis (today called Tbilisi), home of the Theological Seminary, was a bustling railroad town of 150,000, almost twenty times the size of little Gori—and it was brimming with revolutionaries of every stripe.

In those days, the czarist government deported "political undesirables" to remote areas where it was thought they could do no harm. Georgia seemed a safe, faraway dumping ground for this purpose, and it became a hotbed of political exiles from all over Russia.

Some revolutionaries wanted to seize land from the landowners. Others wanted to organize the factory workers. Some hoped for peaceful reform; others were terrorists with bombs under their coats. Police spies (the Okhrana) and stool pigeons were everywhere, gathering information on all of them.

The workers in the railroad shops of Tiflis were prime targets for Marxist revolutionary organizers called Social Democrats (SDs). Many theological students became involved with the SDs, and soon Soso was sneaking out of the seminary to go to SD meetings organized by "old" revolutionary pros (in their twenties). The meetings were held in workers' houses down by the railroad workshops. Odd mixtures of young intellectuals and illiterate workers came together in seminars of a sort in which the revolutionaries preached and taught Marxism to the workers. These young agitators appealed to every side of Soso's personality. They scorned religion, preached a classless society, and predicted a future of power and authority for common people. To Soso Djugashvili they were irresistible. He joined the Tiflis branch of the Social Democratic Party, the party of Lenin.

Soso becomes Koba

By 1900 Soso had left the seminary. The seminary was a six-year school, but Soso was expelled before the end of his fifth year for not taking examinations. He took a position (the only conventional "job" he was ever to have) as an overnight clerk in the Tiflis Astronomical Observatory. The work was light, but it required someone who could read and write and had some education. It paid poorly, however, and no one with better opportunities was interested. The result was that one hard-up rebel or revolutionary after another occupied the post, and Soso was only one of a long line to work at the observatory by night and hurry off to secret revolutionary circles and meetings by day.

In March 1901, the Okhrana mounted a raid in Tiflis. The czar's political police spread a dragnet meant to capture all the members of the Socialist Democratic movement in the city. Djugashvili was on the list, but the police could not find him. Soso had fled the observatory, taken the name Koba, and gone underground. This was the beginning of his life as a professional revolutionary.[3]

A REVOLUTIONARY'S LIFE

To stay out of the clutches of the Okhrana, many Russian revolutionaries, including Lenin, lived abroad. They spent their time studying, speaking, writing, being thrown out of one country and moving to another, living a hand-to-mouth existence in cheap boarding houses. For those like Stalin, who stayed within the borders of Russia, life was even more grueling. It was an existence of hunger, heat, cold, and indifference to all those discomforts. It was a life of hiding out and running away. It meant long sentences in grimy jails and longer periods of exile to frigid isolation in the tundra of Siberia, where temperatures dropped to 70 degrees below freezing in the winter, and hordes of biting gnats drove people and animals frantic in the summer. Above all it was a life of conspiracy—against the government, and against each other as well.

The life of conspiracy came naturally to Soso Djugashvili, now Koba. Experience had taught him to manipulate and deceive people. Even as a little boy he had learned how to dominate his peers by playing one boy off against another.

As soon as Soso joined the Social Democrats, he began the same game. He sowed rumors and tried to turn party members against each other, building up a little band of his own who were troublemakers within the party. But the SD party, a group firmly united in their ideals, had strong morale and a lot of team spirit. They found Soso disruptive and arrogant, and they finally got him out of their hair by booting him out of Tiflis. It was to Batum on the Black Sea that Koba went next, in November 1901.

Batum was a rough-and-tumble oil town, full of bandits and brigands, with an atmosphere of every man for himself. In Batum the party was trying to organize the oil workers, and Koba set out to incite demonstrations and strikes of the workers against their bosses.

Koba was convinced that the ends always justified the means. The great goal of revolution, he said, justified violence, no matter who got hurt or how badly. After a strike at the refineries and a political demonstration (in which Koba probably had a hand) several hundred workers were jailed. Koba used the occasion to organize an enormous march on the jail. He knew perfectly well that the crowd would probably be fired upon. He was frank to say that innocent victims—the more the better—would help to arouse the people more violently against the government and the factory owners.[4]

Iremashvili, Stalin's old schoolmate, said that Sta-

Czar's police mug shot of Stalin with
record of his activities.

lin seemed intoxicated by bloodshed.[5] But it seems he was very careful to protect himself from it. Throughout his life, when there were shootings or violent demonstrations, Stalin stayed on the sidelines. In the dangerous hours of the Bolshevik takeover in 1917, Stalin stayed home. In World War II he was probably the only military commander who never visited the front.[6]

KOBA THE SPY?

The big demonstration in Batum on March 9, 1902, was a disaster. Two thousand workers, incited and urged by Koba against the judgment of party leaders, marched on the jail. Government troops fired. Dozens of marchers and bystanders were killed or wounded, and hundreds of arrests were made. The party lost many of its most effective leaders in Batum.

The Social Democrats were horrified. Even more than the SDs in Tiflis, they were disgusted by the tactics of the violent peasant from Gori who was getting party leaders arrested and innocent people killed. Rumors drifted (not for the first time): could Koba be an *agent provocateur*—an agent in the pay of the police?

The Okhrana hired such people by the hundreds. The *agent provocateur* was paid to provoke people to do something illegal so that they could be arrested. The ranks of all the revolutionary parties were full of police spies, informants, and "moles." You never knew when a trusted comrade would turn out to be an Okhrana agent, waiting for the best moment to turn you in. Typically, an *agent provocateur* would stir up a demonstration or arrange an illegal meeting, and then tip off the police, who would mount a raid and pull in their catch.

Was Stalin a police informant, or wasn't he? It seems impossible to prove one way or another; perfectly sincere revolutionaries did everything an *agent provocateur* did—except inform the police. The fact that Koba kept getting people arrested or shot because of his actions could have been the result of hotheaded enthusiasm rather than betrayal. It is evident that many comrades in 1901 were suspicious of Koba, who never seemed to be wounded or arrested himself. Koba was about to be thrown out of the party in 1902 when the police arrested him for the first time and shut him up in jail for a year and a half before trying him and sentencing him to exile in Siberia.

What makes some biographers suspect that Stalin in those days was a spy is the fact that Stalin was so conveniently whisked away just when things were getting sticky for him in the party. And when dates and details of his years in "exile" are examined and compared, they don't always match, and some seem flatly contradictory.[7]

The matter is of interest chiefly because it would give us some insight into whether Stalin's stubborn pursuit of a "place" in the revolution sprang originally from idealism or from the pursuit of personal power. But hard evidence has never come to light, for Stalin destroyed hundreds of early records as soon as he became powerful enough to do so (see Chapter 8).

CHAPTER 3

THE REVOLUTIONARIES

Fifteen years passed between the time twenty-three-year-old Djugashvili became Koba the revolutionary and the Revolution itself in 1917. In those years Koba grew from a young fire-eating rebel to a mustachioed, hardened veteran. He was not yet a leader, but he came to the attention of V.I. Lenin, who would be called the Father of the Revolution. These years also saw the rise of another man, one who would become Stalin's greatest enemy—Leon Trotsky. Ironically, Trotsky helped Lenin to create the dictatorship that Stalin ultimately took over.

LENIN AND TROTSKY

During the making of the Russian Revolution, Lenin and Trotsky were far more important than Stalin. They were idealists motivated, as Trotsky wrote, by sympathy for the oppressed. They were also zealots in the grip of an overriding idea—the workers' state.

Lenin and Trotsky were not peaceful men; they did not wish to wait for Marx's "forces of history" to change the world. Although their motives were unselfish, they were prepared to use every kind of violence in the name of the Revolution. They recoiled from the injustice of the czar's regime and the misery of the masses. (It is a measure of how big the oppressed populations were that the very poor were always referred to as "the masses.") The parents of Lenin and Trotsky, however, were neither poor nor oppressed. Only Stalin came from a childhood of poverty and an ancestry of serfdom.

Lenin was a hereditary noble. He was short and bald and always looked as if he had slept in his clothes. (Often he had.) He had high cheekbones and piercing slanted eyes inherited from Tartar ancestors. People who met him mentioned those eyes as "merry" and "twinkling" (in contrast, so Trotsky said, to Stalin's evil "yellow eyes"). Lenin's charm and intelligence dazzled people. One friend said, "I had the feeling he could see ten feet into the earth."[1]

Trotsky, who was Stalin's age, was the son of a hardworking, prosperous farmer. (He was a Jew, which did not endear him to Stalin, who grew more and more anti-Semitic through the years.) Both Lenin and Trotsky were intellectuals, "deep thinkers." They lived in libraries; they wrote thousands of pages of theory, history, biography—even while they were organizing revolutionary groups and directing revolutionary projects. They spent years abroad and spoke several languages. They were comfortable in high-flown discussions of theory; Stalin was silent and ill at ease. They were sophisticated and cosmopolitan; Stalin was awkward. (Trotsky called him vulgar, coarse, and mean.) Lenin and Trotsky were hypnotic speakers who drew crowds to their flashing oratory; Stalin was a poor Georgian speaker who spoke Russian with a thick accent.

Either Lenin or Trotsky could easily have become a respectable, well-off family man, living a comfortable life and discussing politics at ease at the dinner table. Stalin's only way out of servitude was the church or the Revolution. Despite their differences, all three became Marxist revolutionaries and members of the Social Democratic party.

"GIVE US AN ORGANIZATION OF REVOLUTIONARIES AND WE WILL OVERTURN RUSSIA!"—V. I. Lenin[2]

From the very beginning the Social Democrats fought among themselves. Should they try to reform the present regime or must they destroy it? Should they use violence? Terrorism? If so, how much? Should the party be broad and democratic, or small, elite, tightly organized?

Lenin was a man of organized mind. To bring about a revolution, he insisted, two things were necessary: a tightly disciplined group under a small, elite central committee, and a party whose membership would be restricted to professional revolutionaries. (Both of these conditions would help to give Stalin his chance to accumulate power.)

The majority of party members, which included Trotsky, wanted a large, democratic organization with room for compromise, where decisions would be made by majority vote. Trotsky instantly saw the danger in Lenin's idea and opposed it right up to the Revolution. He said: "The organization of the party takes the place of the party itself; the central committee takes the place of the organization, and finally the dictator takes the place of the central committee."[3] That was exactly what happened.

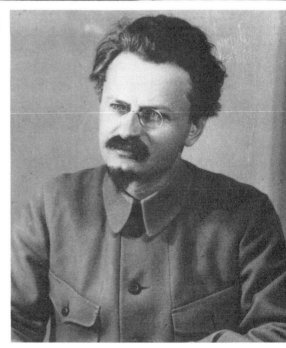

Stalin and Lenin (top);
Trotsky (bottom).

When the Marxist revolutionaries took power in Russia, the "dictatorship of the proletariat" quickly became the dictatorship of the party, and then, to a terrifying degree, the dictatorship of Stalin himself.

BOLSHEVIKS AND MENSHEVIKS

When the SD party finally split for good, Lenin accomplished a smart public relations move. He won a minor issue by two or three votes and took to calling his own group "Bolsheviks," which means "majority." The Bolsheviks were in fact a very small minority. The other group, with a much larger membership, found themselves saddled for all time with the name "Menshevik," which means "minority." These inappropriate titles lasted until Lenin renamed his party "Communists" after the Revolution.

Trotsky aligned himself loosely with the Mensheviks, but Stalin took his time deciding which side of the SDs to favor. The two factions of the SDs fought so bitterly it was like a religious war. In the end, Stalin went with Lenin. He didn't trust "the people," and democracy was not to his taste. Lenin's view that people must be led was more hardheaded and unsentimental and suited him better. Besides, in a small, organized party he might have the greater chance of an important role in the future. Once Stalin had made his choice, he threw himself into Lenin's cause. He developed a hatred for the opposition that never left him and added to his enmity for Trotsky.

In the end, Trotsky, too, joined the small and disciplined Bolshevik Party that seized power in Russia in 1917. It was ironic that Trotsky helped Lenin to set the stage for the dictatorship of Stalin, his most hated enemy.

WAR WITH JAPAN

While the Social Democratic Party was fighting itself, Russia was engaged in a war with Japan. The war led to a spontaneous and doomed revolution that broke out in 1905 without the help of any organized party. The Bolsheviks didn't take part, but the events were important because they prepared the ground for the 1917 Revolution and pushed the nation to its final crisis.

The Russo-Japanese War had to do with the czar's ambitions in Korea and Manchuria. Czar Nicholas II was confident that Russia's might could handle the Japanese without difficulty. He could acquire some new territory and at the same time give people at home something to think about besides revolt and revolution. Throughout history, governments have found war a useful way of distracting the public. However, the czar's luck and judgment misfired once again.

The Japanese mounted a surprise attack on Port Arthur, a Russian fort in the Yellow Sea, where they bottled up the Russian fleet. The czar's planning and strategy were disastrous. Nothing was done right, and nothing went right. The czar's court kept interfering with the strategy of the generals. The garrison at Port Arthur starved. Bungling and waste were the order of the day. No one could believe what was happening—not the czar, not the Russian people, not the rest of Europe. The Japanese won one battle after another. Patriotic fervor soon evaporated, and on September 5, 1905, a humiliating peace agreement was signed. The Russian people were filled with shame and anger. Their sons had been sent to die in a fruitless war to satisfy the vanity of the czar. And now the "bony hand of hunger" gripped the population.

BLOOD UPON THE SNOW (1905)

> "I cried out to them 'Stand up!' but they lay still,
> their arms stretched out lifelessly, and the scarlet
> stain of blood upon the snow."—**Father Gapon**[4]

In the capital city of St. Petersburg in 1905, there
was no bread, no food, no fuel for heat. People had
learned to do without meat, but in Russia bread is
the staff of life. With no bread to be had at the
bakeries, housewives went on a rampage. The
workers took up the cry. The city was in an uproar.

A popular, charismatic, but naive priest called
Father Gapon decided to lead the workers of St.
Petersburg in a mammoth, peaceful march to present a petition to the czar. The requests of the
workers were reasonable, Gapon assured them; the
czar, their "Little Father," would understand and
grant their wishes over the heads of his corrupt
ministers. Gapon dutifully announced his intention
to the police and explained that the crowd would be
peaceful and unarmed. The czar was terrified. He
took his family and went "on vacation," leaving his
generals, police, and troops in charge of the palace.

The scene that followed went down in history as
"Bloody Sunday." On a Sunday morning in 1905,
more than 200,000 men, women, and children gathered to present their petition. No weapons were
carried. Religious pictures were held aloft to show
reverence, as were pictures of the czar. Crosses were
everywhere, and the marchers sang "God save the
czar!" as they moved toward the palace. On this
huge, unarmed, and humble crowd, the czar's
troops opened fire. The mounted Cossacks wielded
their whips and sabers; "The swords rose and fell,"[5]
said Father Gapon, weeping. Screaming women
cowered over their children.

The troops spread out, surrounding the people and firing point blank into their ranks. People lay in the snow in their blood or tried to run or crouched over the wounded to protect them. "Bloody Sunday" killed the old, powerful, sentimental feelings the people had felt for their czar. Father Gapon called down a curse—"Be thou damned!"—on the head of the ruler he had thought of as the Little Father of the Russian people; "Oh soul destroyer," he raged, "may all the blood that must be shed fall upon thee and thy kindred."[6]

CHAPTER 4

REVOLT AND WAR
(1905–1917)

A major revolt against the czar followed Bloody
Sunday in 1905. The revolt was unsuccessful, but it
was a prelude to the great revolution twelve years
later. It showed what could be done. Lenin himself
viewed 1905 as a rehearsal for the real thing, and he
put down his books on Marxist theory to study
tactics of street fighting and how to make bombs.

THE PRACTICE REVOLUTION

The 1905 uprising was not organized by any party;
it was a true popular revolt. Waves of strikes paralyzed the country. Bombs were tossed like bou-
quets. Officials were assassinated right and left.
Peasants seized land and burned down the manor
houses of the landlords. Factory workers organized
themselves into "soviets," or councils. Soviets were
elected in every city. Stalin's future enemy Trotsky
was in the forefront, in the first soviet in St. Petersburg. (In 1918, with his slogan, "All power to

the Soviets," Lenin would make the soviets the basic units of revolution, and they remain the basic administrative units of the USSR today.)

Abroad, Europe and the United States were sympathetic to the uprising, so obvious was the corruption of the czar's regime. Czar Nicholas saw finally that he would have to pacify his angry people somehow. In October he agreed to a Duma, or parliament, and a constitution, and the revolt subsided for the moment. The Duma wasn't much of a parliament, however, but more like a channel for polite advice with no powers of its own. The czar soon cracked down, using the momentary lull to subdue his rebellious people. Government troops with their firing squads, and cossacks on horseback with their whips and swords, put down the resistance in the countryside. Reactionary, anti-Semitic thugs sowed violence against Jews and intellectuals. These anti-Semites called themselves the Union of the Russian People, but they came down in history as "The Black Hundreds." The Duma continued to meet at intervals, but the "practice revolution" was over.

WORLD WAR I (1914)

During all this time, the revolutionary parties were in fragments, fighting each other more than the government. In terms of organized action, everything hung fire. Lenin, moping in Paris, was downhearted, and sighed that he would never live to see the Revolution.

Then, off in Bosnia (now Yugoslavia), the Archduke Ferdinand of Austria was assassinated, lighting the spark that set off World War I. It was this war that finally shook Czar Nicholas from his throne.

Czar Nicholas had his usual blind hopes about

war; war with Germany would unite the Russian people and get them off his back. But this war was even more of a disaster for the czar than the Japanese war of 1904. As usual, the transportation system wasn't able to get arms and supplies where they were needed. The czar's "military might" turned out to be flesh and blood, not rifles and artillery. At the front, hundreds of thousands of peasant soldiers were forced simply to rush at the enemy—sometimes barehanded—and were mowed down.

The dismayed but physically brave czar departed for the front, and the government was left to his wife and her chosen advisor, a crazed and crafty "monk" called Rasputin. Thoughtful and intelligent ministers were fired and lightweights whom Rasputin could manipulate were installed. While Russia starved, the social life of the elite went on with only a few inconveniences. There were hunting parties, fancy balls, silks, satins, fine wines, and French cooks.

For the common people there was still a grave shortage of food and fuel. The machinery of government sputtered and ground to a halt. The country found itself on the brink of total breakdown. Finally, in Petrograd (previously called St. Petersburg), the Duma and the Petrograd soviet took over the capital, and on March 2, 1917, Czar Nicholas was forced to abdicate.

WHERE WAS KOBA?

What was Joseph Djugashvili, alias Koba, doing during these fateful years? The details of his life from 1904 to the Revolution of 1917 are obscure. We know many things he was involved in, but not always how big or small a part he played. Trotsky says that he worked behind the scenes, selecting people for party projects, giving them authorizations from the party, and then fading from the picture. A few historians think he was working for the czar's secret police.

The biographies that were approved by Stalin after he became "Stalin the All-Wise" have him in seven places at once, larger than life, leading strikes, organizing revolutionary groups, founding Bolshevik newspapers—popular, beloved, and revered by his comrades. In fact, however, he did not play a major role in the party until after the Revolution.

For many of these years Koba was either in prison or in exile. The jails in those days were "open," in the sense that prisoners were not in cells but could move around within the prison. By an unwritten rule, political prisoners kept themselves apart from criminals. But Koba left the other "politicals" to their gossip and arguments on theory and went off to hobnob with the thugs, forgers, and thieves in another part of the prison. He could talk their language and, as he said, he admired people who "knew how to do things."

In exile it was the same story; cast out into a lonely village of a few smoky, roach-infested huts on the frozen tundra, more than one exile committed suicide out of loneliness and despair. When there was a group, they depended on one another's companionship. Fellow exiles found Koba sly, cold, and distant. He was certainly not "one of the boys," swapping bits of news or arguing Marxist theory with the rest. Koba kept to himself, setting traps and fishing for food with a small dog for company.

When he wasn't jailed or in exile, Koba spent most of his time drumming up membership for the Bolsheviks back in the Caucasus (a territory located between the Caspian and the Black seas) where the Mensheviks were strong. To them he became "the most hated of the Bolsheviks"[1] for his tireless war against them by fair means or foul—mostly foul, it seems. This, coupled with his energy and persistence, established Koba's credentials with the Bolsheviks, and at the end of 1905 he was invited to a party conference in Finland.

There, he met Lenin in person for the first time and was startled to find the "mountain eagle" to be a small, squarish person in a baggy suit. He soon realized that Lenin's bulging forehead held a brain not only of extraordinary intelligence but of hard-headed resolve much more appealing to Koba than any "soft" ideas about bloodless revolutions, parliaments, or "liberal reform."

Hardness, in fact, was a quality the Bolsheviks prized, and many of them took names to symbolize it; Vyacheslav Skriabin, later foreign minister of the USSR, took the name Molotov, which means "hammer." The inappropriate name of the good-natured, cautious Lev Kamenev means "stony." And Koba, as we know, took the name Stalin, meaning "steely," or made of steel.

Lenin despised the very notion of "reform." To him the word "reform" was just a cover for the middle classes' grab for power. He wanted to destroy the whole system. He warned the party and the workers against spending their energies on getting better wages or working conditions. He called that "economism." If the economic struggle took center stage, the *social* revolution, the *class* revolution would never happen. He explained this tirelessly, keeping his revolutionary eye trained on the great historic goals.

Koba, too, wanted to see the system destroyed, and he had a further reason for turning his back on the liberals and moderates. Many of them were the very men and women who so looked down on him for his peasant crudeness, his violence, and his lack of polish.

LENIN AND STALIN

Most of the revolutionary leaders were not peasants or factory workers themselves. But Koba *was* a man of the people. Lenin saw several possibilities in such a man. Koba had intelligence and some education. He understood the political game; yet he could talk to the rough, uneducated workers in their own salty vocabulary, trading crude jokes, cursing the bosses, and boiling down the complicated theories of Karl Marx into a simple brew, easy to digest.

Lenin was also attracted by Koba's cool acceptance of the notion that the Bolsheviks should use criminal methods—especially to get money. The party was always hard up. It was expensive to print illegal papers, support the party members, send comrades from place to place, and pay bribes to police agents.

Lenin had come to the conclusion that it could be justified to steal from the rich (the government) and give to the poor (the party). He called such actions "expropriations," or "exes," a more tactful word than robbery or heist. The Mensheviks, and many Bolsheviks, too, rejected robbery and violence that left innocent victims in its wake. (The tougher revolutionaries called them "vegetarians.")

But Koba considered innocent victims a useful spur to revolutionary anger among the people. Lenin and Stalin had this in common: both subscribed to the classic rationalization, "You can't make an omelette without breaking eggs," or as they put it, "You can't make a revolution wearing silk gloves." Lenin now took this dangerous youth under his wing.

With Lenin's secret approval, Koba took part in organizing a campaign of crime in the Caucasus. A protection racket was set up, run by criminals who shared the loot. Bolshevik conspirators robbed banks and post offices. The Mensheviks were appalled and disgusted. They had outlawed criminal methods. They blamed Koba, especially, for an infamous robbery and shooting in Tiflis. It aroused such a furor of criticism that in later years, when Stalin had his own version of prerevolutionary events recorded, he couldn't seem to make up his mind whether or not to take credit for any of the "exes."

Lenin saw yet another advantage in having Koba in the Bolshevik camp: Koba was not Russian, but Georgian. Lenin wanted the support of the "nationalities" (the national minorities), but the Bolsheviks were mostly Great Russians. How could they hope to convince people, such as the Poles, who hated everything Russian, to join them? (It was not to be easily solved; the nationalities are a major problem for the Soviet government to this day.)

Lenin saw that Koba could be of real help. He suggested that Koba study the problem. The words and ideas of "the wonderful Georgian,"[2] as Lenin called Stalin in a burst of appreciation, would bear more weight with the national minorities than those of any Great Russian.

Stalin, ever practical, devised a practical approach: promise them anything. He pointed out, quite correctly, that the nationalities were struggling mainly against each other, which would get them nowhere while they were under the yoke of the czar. They must throw their combined weight with the Party to overthrow the czar. Once that was done, the new Russian federation would guarantee the independent rights of all the nationalities, and they would have no reason to leave the federation.

Koba laid out this argument in a somewhat stodgy piece of writing entitled *Marxism and the National Question,* published in 1913. It was this and his own non-Russian birth that eventually landed Koba with the job of commissar of nationalities in the new Bolshevik government after the Revolution. It was the job that put him on the powerful Central Committee of the Bolshevik party.

KOBA'S MARRIAGE

Sometime during the turbulent years surrounding the 1905 revolution—probably in 1904—Koba married a Georgian girl, Ekaterina Svanidze. They had a son, Yakov, whom Koba handed over to relatives after his wife's death, and whom he treated with contempt after he came into power.

Koba's young wife was a gentle, submissive girl who suited him well. Ekaterina served him, and prayed for him, but she never injected her own opinions or asserted herself. This was the Georgian way. Elsewhere, women were full participants among the revolutionaries. They were writers and activists; some were terrorists. Their names fill the histories of the Revolution. But Stalin was never able to see a woman as an equal partner. Years later, he told one of his sons that intellectual women were nothing but skinny "herrings with ideas."[3] Ekaterina—soft, admiring, and obedient—soothed his prickly sense that everyone else looked down on him. She adored him. His old friend Iremashvili said she treated Soso as a demigod.

Ekaterina died only a few years after their marriage, probably around 1910. Iremashvili came to her funeral, and Soso told him of the desolation he felt. His words are quoted in many works about Stalin for their poignancy and their prophetic sense: "This creature softened my stony heart," he said. "She has died, and with her my last warm feelings for all human beings have died."[4]

THE BOLSHEVIK REVOLUTION (1917)

The devastation of World War I led to the Russian Revolution of 1917. It was a revolution in two parts. The first part began with the uprising in Petrograd (today called Leningrad) in March and ended with the abdication of the czar and the formation of a provisional government. The second part came in November when the Bolsheviks seized power and Communist Russia was born.

When the czar was forced to step down, the old Duma formed a provisional, or temporary, government. Plans were made to elect a Constituent Assembly that would draw up a constitution for the new Russian republic. Amnesty was declared for all political prisoners, including Stalin, who had spent the war years in Siberia. In March 1917, Stalin boarded the train for St. Petersburg, which by now had changed its name to Petrograd because it sounded more Russian. ("Burg," after all, was the German word for city, and the Germans were the enemy.)

Stalin set off with high hopes. He arrived with

Lev Kamenev ("Stony"), who had been a fellow exile in Siberia. They were the first members of the Bolshevik Central Committee to arrive in Petrograd. Lenin was cooling his heels in frustration in Zurich, Switzerland. Trotsky was biting his nails on 164th Street in New York. For the Bolsheviks, no one was minding the store, except for a small Party Bureau.

In Petrograd, Stalin found himself as unpopular as ever. The local Bolshevik Bureau rejected him; they didn't like "certain personal traits of his." Stalin reacted by asserting himself. He and Kamenev were the only Central Committee members in Petrograd, and they had seniority. They marched into the offices of *Pravda,* the Party newspaper, and booted out the editor, who happened to be Vyacheslav Molotov, "the hammer." (Molotov would hold high posts in the Party and outlive them all.) Stalin and Kamenev became joint editors, and now they had to decide what line to take.

IN PETROGRAD

Petrograd in March 1917 was in a state of wild disarray. There was a combination of excitement and misery. Food and fuel were still in severely short supply. Politically, no one could decide who should run the show. The provisional government was made up mostly of middle-class, reform-minded liberals and socialists who remained faithful to the allies fighting the Germans.

Meeting in the same building with the provisional government was the leadership of the Petrograd soviet, or council of workers. The soviet included Bolsheviks, Mensheviks, and a large group of Social Revolutionaries representing a strange mix of peasants, shopkeepers, soldiers, and workers. The soviet couldn't make up its collective mind about what it wanted and what to do next; should it trust the promises of the provisional government? And what about the war? Even the military was divided on that. Everyone wanted to see the Germans beaten, but the war was taking a dreadful toll on the Russians. Lenin, writing from abroad, laid out the Bolshevik position: get out of the war and don't accept the provisional government. But the Bolsheviks were only a small group within the Petrograd soviet, and they didn't have much clout.

In the Bolshevik newspaper, *Pravda*, Stalin and Kamenev began to lean toward bargaining with the provisional government. It was absolutely against Lenin's ideas. To Lenin the provisional government was just a front for the bourgeois liberals who would sabotage the Revolution. The war, he said, was just another capitalist enterprise waged for the benefit of international businesses, arms manufacturers, and colony-grabbing empires.

To the practical-minded Stalin, however, the provisional government simply looked like the best bet—the organization most likely to win and keep the power of government. Negotiating with the provisional government seemed the only way for the Bolshevik minority to gain power. He began to tone down Lenin's articles in *Pravda*. Lenin, reading smuggled editions of *Pravda* in Zurich, was infuriated; but he was 2,000 miles away from Petrograd.

Neither Stalin nor Kamenev had any way of knowing at this point that Lenin, impossibly, would bob up from exile, turn Petrograd on its head, and in a few months seize power once and for all against incredible odds.

LENIN RETURNS

While Stalin was being cautious in Petrograd, Lenin was anxious to get out of "this damned Switzerland" and back to Russia through all the war zones.

In a peculiar twist of history, it was the German enemy that provided the way. If Russia got out of the war, Germany would be able to concentrate her troops against the Western allies. The German command decided that perhaps Lenin could be the one to get Russia out of the war.

The German government offered Lenin safe and secret passage across Germany to Russia in a special train. The train was completely sealed, its windows boarded up, and no stops were to be made. In the image conjured up by Winston Churchill, then Britain's minister of war, the Germans "turned upon Russia the most grisly of all weapons. They transported Lenin in a sealed truck like a plague bacillus from Switzerland into Russia."[1]

In April 1917 Lenin arrived at the Finland Station in Petrograd. It was a dramatic moment in history. Thousands of Bolshevik workers and soldiers were there; the members of the Petrograd soviet were there. Friends and foes alike—everyone came to see Lenin step off the train.

Everyone except Stalin. He knew that Lenin would not be pleased with him, and he wanted to let the dust settle before he decided what to do next. In Trotsky's words, during those days Stalin just became still, "waiting cautiously, peering about," trying to size up the situation.[2] Later, however, in his "official" histories, Stalin looms large in the greeting at the Finland Station. Doctored photographs put him prominently at the scene, but in fact he was not there.

Crowds of workers and soldiers filled the square in front of the station. Bands played revolutionary anthems, including the French anthem, *The Marseillaise:* "The day of glory has come! . . . The blood-stained flag is raised!

But in fact, until Lenin spoke, none of that huge mixed crowd was considering further revolution.

Lenin was an impassioned orator who drew crowds every time he spoke.

People wanted things to settle down. The czar was gone, and now they wanted to get on with it and build a stable government. That would achieve a *political* revolution.

The *social* revolution seemed to be forgotten, but not by Lenin. He was lifted to the top of an armored car, and made a speech that stunned the crowd. He spoke to the workers and peasants of their historic destiny. The peasants must seize the land; the workers must take over the factories; the provisional government was a capitalist tool and must be destroyed. The Bolsheviks must never compromise.

Lenin got a wild ovation, but people were looking at one another as if to say, "Is he *serious*?" It took him several months of talking, but Lenin *was* serious, and in the end he won over much of the Petrograd soviet. And Stalin once more became his devoted follower.

The month after Lenin's triumphant return, Trotsky struggled back to Russia from New York. He arrived in May, and he too joined Lenin and the Bolsheviks. Trotsky and Stalin took an instant dislike to one another, but without Trotsky, the Bolshevik Revolution could never have succeeded. People crowded the halls to hear Trotsky speak. He was a brilliant strategist and it was he, not Stalin, who became Lenin's right hand. Between them, Lenin and Trotsky took over the Revolution and created the Communist dictatorship that followed. Between them they unknowingly prepared the way for Stalin.

A "GRAY BLUR" BECOMES A COMMISSAR

The provisional government was by now thoroughly alarmed and set out to arrest Bolsheviks where it could find them. Through all the secret meetings of Bolshevik leaders, where danger and excitement were high and policy and action were being ham-

mered out, Stalin was almost invisible. A reporter
in Petrograd said Stalin in those days produced "the
impression of a gray blur, looming up now and then
dimly, not leaving any trace."[3]

On November 4 Stalin was present at a secret all-
night meeting called by Lenin (disguised in a wig)
when the dangerous decision was made: the Bolsheviks would attempt to overthrow the provisional
government in an armed uprising. The next night,
Stalin stayed home while the Bolsheviks met in a
white heat of excitement to mobilize the Red Guard
and prepare for the attack. That night Stalin stayed
home, quietly sipping tea with the parents of his
future wife, Nadezhda Alliluyev.

On November 7, 1917, under Trotsky's direction,
Lenin and the Bolsheviks seized power in Petrograd.
They took the bridges and strategic streets and buildings. At dawn they stormed the government building, the Winter Palace, and ousted the provisional
government in an almost bloodless coup.

In his guttural voice, rolling his Rs, Lenin announced coolly, "We shall now proceed to construct
the new Socialist order."[4] It was a thrilling moment
for the idealistic revolutionaries. But in the end,
Lenin's Revolution constructed a dictatorship more
absolute and more ruthless than that of any czar.

The Bolsheviks now formed a cabinet of fifteen
members to run the government until the planned
Constituent Assembly could draw up a new constitution. The title "minister" had a czarist ring to
Lenin's ears so he called the new cabinet members
"commissars." The names were called out in the
weary small hours of the morning of November 8,
1917. Lenin was president; Trotsky was commissar
for foreign affairs; the last one on the list was "I.V.
Djugashvili, commissar for nationalities."[5] It was an
unimportant office, but it was Stalin's foothold on
the ladder to power.

CHAPTER 6

ONE PARTY RULES THE STATE

Stalin did not start the rule of one party over the nation; Lenin, Trotsky, and the Civil War did.

The Bolsheviks, carrying Stalin along like a twig on the flood, had seized the Winter Palace; but they were far from secure. Their support had grown, but so had their enemies. Lenin's slogans, "Bread, Peace, Land! Freedom!," had brought him the support of workers, soldiers, and peasants, but there wasn't any bread, and there wasn't any peace, and the city was a picture of violence and chaos.

A stream of decrees had been issued by Lenin. Private ownership of land was abolished; non-Bolshevik newspapers were suppressed; private trade and business were banned. Lenin sent armed squads into the countryside to seize grain, for in Petrograd the bread ration was down to two ounces a day.

By December Lenin had created the Cheka, a new political police more formidable than the czar's

Okhrana. "Do you think we can be victors without the most severe revolutionary terror?" Lenin said impatiently. The Cheka began to impose Bolshevik policy by force. The middle class was already against the Bolsheviks, and now the peasants and many of the other revolutionaries and reformers turned against them too.

THE BOLSHEVIKS
HANG ON

In January 1918, the promised Constituent Assembly was elected to form the new government. The Bolsheviks found themselves soundly defeated. They won only about one fourth of the seats, and most of the other delegates wanted to get rid of them, their crazy programs, and their terrorist tactics.

Once more the Bolsheviks took the offensive. Their armed supporters surrounded the convention hall. Bolshevik rowdies drowned out the speeches and resolutions of the assembly with catcalls, whistles, and shrieks. Finally at two in the morning an armed sailor of the Bolshevik guard turned out the lights and firmly sent the members away with the simple phrase: "The guard is tired."[1]

Once in control, almost the first move of the Bolsheviks was to get Russia out of World War I. In March 1918 the Bolsheviks signed the Treaty of Brest-Litovsk and pulled Russia's troops out of the war.

The treaty gave up large chunks of the Russian Empire, including the Baltic states, Finland, Poland, and the Ukraine. This expensive treaty angered a great many Russians—and of course it angered Russia's former allies who counted on Russia to continue fighting Germany.

A rare print of the Bolshevik Red Guard in front of the Winter Palace, Petrograd. They were civilians organized and armed by Trotsky.

WAR AGAIN (1918–1921)

The Bolsheviks took Russia out of World War I, but what followed was the Russian Civil War, the Bolshevik (Communist) "Reds" against the anti-Communist "Whites." Against the Reds, it seemed, was the rest of the world: former generals of the czar, socialists, liberals, foreign troops, and—last but not least—national minorities, which were setting up their own independent governments. The British, French, and Americans sent money, arms, and men to fight the Reds.

The Civil War forced the Bolsheviks to make the structure of the Party even more rigid than before. They were a small embattled minority surrounded by enthusiastic enemies, so they had to be organized and commanded like an army. Lenin was commander-in-chief, but the two who helped him build the system were mutual enemies, Stalin and Trotsky.

Trotsky recruited a ragtag bunch of soldiers, workers, and peasants; armed them, trained them, terrorized them; and forged the mighty Red Army. Stalin was put in charge of gouging grain out of the reluctant peasants.

WAR COMMUNISM

To hold off economic collapse and win the war, Lenin set up an emergency program called "War Communism." For Stalin it was like a rehearsal. The government took over the whole economy and set out to build its industrial power fast. To feed the workers, grain was to be "donated" by the peasants—that is, given willingly or confiscated by force. Stalin's men roamed the country raiding the villages, and "Stalin's trains" carried grain to the cities rioting for bread.

Villagers during the Civil War found themselves caught in the middle. If they refused to help one side, they were shot. If they did give help, the other side came and shot them later. They were like the victims of civil war anywhere.

The firing squads of the "Red Terror" executed up to 50,000 people during the Civil War. The Whites, "The White Terror," killed even more. In one short, three-month period, the Whites liquidated almost 100,000 Finnish workers.

The Whites began with the upper hand. The Reds held the center, but surrounding them, the Whites occupied major industrial centers and the grain-producing areas; and they held the railroad. An Allied blockade kept supplies from reaching the Reds. But the Whites were disorganized. They fought one another almost as much as they fought the Reds. They behaved like many small armies, each out to line its own pockets with power, land, or loot. They had no common strategy or goal. The Reds had Lenin, the dominating mind of the Revolution, and Trotsky, the brilliant head of a tightly (and very ruthlessly) disciplined army.

THE GENERAL SECRETARY

When the Civil War came to an end in December of 1920, the country was again in the throes of starvation and ruin, but the Red Army had won the war. Russia became the Union of Soviet Socialist Republics, and the Bolsheviks renamed themselves the Communist party. The Soviet Union had become a one-party, Communist state.

Lenin dictated policy and controlled the whole; Trotsky continued as commander of the Red Army.

And Stalin? Except for a few military forays that increased Trotsky's contempt, Stalin did the "office work."

It was Lenin's idea. He needed a practical manager, and Stalin was efficient and didn't talk a lot. Lenin appointed Stalin general secretary of the Central Committee of the Communist party. He was in charge of hiring and firing. He got things done. He was incredibly hardworking and organized. No task was too great or too small. Stalin was on the Politburo (the political bureau) and the Orgburo (the organization bureau). He was the commissar of nationalities and the commissar of inspections (an obscure but powerful job, which allowed him to seek out inefficiency or disloyalty anywhere and everywhere). Stalin was competent, reliable, and invaluable; but no one realized that he was also very dangerous.

ORGANIZING THE PARTY

In 1921 Russia had a population of 140 million people but only one-tenth of one percent were members of the Communist party. How could so few rule so many?

Lenin organized the system that Stalin would take over. It is easy to forget that the Communist dictatorship was not Stalin's child, but Lenin's. By a vote of the Party Congress in 1921, dissenting groups were outlawed within the Party. That was a rule that made orderly change difficult, if not impossible. In 1922, boatloads and trainloads of intellectuals were deported, most of them members of the other revolutionary parties. Scientists, philosophers, writers, people who had an independent turn of mind were asked to leave. Many left without waiting to be asked. Censorship of art and literature was set up under a special arm of government (although it was mild compared to Stalin's censorship to come).

In the system that Lenin built, power was concentrated at the top in the Politburo (short for political bureau). Its members were chosen by the Central Committee of the Communist party. The Central Committee was elected by a Congress of Party representatives from the local Party organizations. (It is worth noting that when Stalin took over, he gradually stopped assembling the Party Congress; thirteen years elapsed between the 17th and 18th Party Congresses.)

It was the Politburo that decided government policy and direction. Including Lenin, the Politburo had only seven members, and Stalin was one of them. Trotsky was another. Kamenev, Stalin's old comrade and coeditor of *Pravda*, was a member and so was Gregory Zinoviev, who would soon save Stalin from a political disaster. Prime Minister Alexei Rykov, and Nikolai Bukharin, the zestful current editor of *Pravda*, made up the doomed group; after Lenin's death, Stalin would get rid of them one by one.

Party members held all the important posts in industry, the army, and the police. Management-level positions were also filled from the Party membership. At the bottom were the Party "cells," small groups, each with a leader. Cells were formed wherever people lived and worked. Cell leaders doled out rewards and punishments, jobs, apartments, favors, and advice to the general population.

Stalin's job as general secretary was to organize all this. When it was created, no one thought of the Secretariat as any more than a "technical" organ of the Party; it was the personnel department, and Stalin was the invisible man who ran it. Lenin and

Trotsky were famous throughout the country, but Stalin was a shadowy figure, unknown to the public. In meetings he sat quietly and seldom spoke. Sometimes he even got bored and left. He never put himself forward.

"EVERYTHING DEPENDS ON 'PERSONNEL' "—**Stalin**[2]

Behind the scenes, as commissar of nationalities and as head of the Secretariat, Stalin was able to build his power base. He set up a group of advisers that came to be called "Comrade Stalin's Private Secretariat." They were more than advisers, however; they ran a network of spies for their boss. Party members all the way down the line were encouraged to collect information on their fellow members above or below. Soon Stalin had bulging dossiers, thousands upon thousands of files on everyone in the Party.

On the basis of all this secret information he planted his own people in the grass-roots cells, in the army, and in the high posts of the secret police.

Had you been heard to praise Trotsky? Mysteriously you were passed over for promotion or sent to some remote province—a desert or a swamp or someplace cold—on a minor job. Did you complain about those bureaucrats in Moscow? Your "disloyalty" would cost you. Did you find yourself in a position of authority? It was made clear to you why you had been chosen, and to whom you owed your good fortune.

The most important point of all was this: *the heads of local Party organs were chosen from a list made up by the office of the general secretary.* This fact alone led to a situation in which the Secretariat, in a roundabout way, elected itself (see flow chart, p. 62). Stalin called it "democratic centralism."

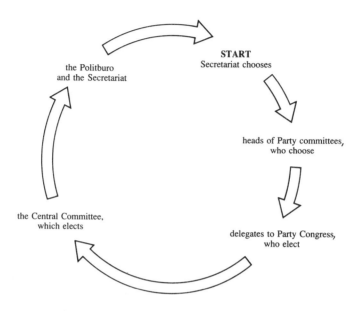

the Politburo
and the Secretariat

START
Secretariat chooses

heads of Party committees,
who choose

delegates to Party Congress,
who elect

the Central Committee,
which elects

In the Politburo, Lenin and Trotsky were occupied with great issues and present dangers. Lenin thought of Stalin as a godsend, taking care of endless details. Trotsky, who found Stalin repellent, thought of him as a useful nobody. At this point no one noticed just how much power was within the grasp of the general secretary.

THE CHEKA

Under the pressures of the Civil War, the kinds of leaders that emerged had to be people who would not flinch from cruel measures and who understood the use of terror. "Violence is the essence of revolution,"[3] argued Lenin.

Like Stalin, Lenin felt that any means were justified to save the Revolution, which meant keeping the Communist party in power. It was especially necessary to put down "enemies of the Revolution," such as reformers, capitalists, and bourgeois folk and the members of other (now outlawed) revolutionary groups. To enforce its will, the government relied on an institution that later swelled like yeast dough under Stalin's rule. It was the Cheka, which grew out of an earlier institution—the Okhrana, the czar's secret police. Cheka stood for the "All Russian Commission for the Suppression of Counter-Revolution and Sabotage," but its shorter name was the "Red Terror."

The Cheka had license to arrest, imprison, and execute any "counter-revolutionary" without trial. It supervised and managed the labor camps and supplied the firing squads.

Dictatorship, argued Lenin, was the necessary stage before the coming of the true stateless, classless society. The other parties were tools of capitalism, he said, and as for Russian workers, they had "insufficient class-consciousness" to understand the historic forces at work. The Party itself must carry out the great design, and must do it by force. The Cheka was the iron fist of the dictatorship.

CHAPTER 7

STALIN HOLDS ON

Lenin was the most powerful and revered symbol of the Revolution, but his style was to persuade, not to dictate. In the Politburo, where everyone had his say, Lenin had to win agreement. He had to argue, discuss, persuade. He was as much a leader as a dictator. For Lenin the Party was everything; it embodied the Revolution. In 1929 Stalin would become the Party.

During 1922 and 1923, less than a year after Stalin's appointment as general secretary, Lenin suffered a series of strokes. Each stroke disabled him a little more. He began to rely more and more on Trotsky to speak for him at the Politburo. A close bond between Lenin and Trotsky was a great danger for Stalin; it would put his worst enemy in a very powerful position.

STALIN AND TROTSKY

The feud between Stalin and Trotsky lasted over twenty years. Not only did they dislike each other

64

from the moment they met in 1913, they clashed on everything—the peasants, the military, the nationalities. While Lenin was alive he stood between them, holding them apart like a referee between two boxers. Trotsky would write to Lenin: "I insist on the removal of Stalin!" Stalin would ask the Central Committee to take the Red Army out of Trotsky's command. Trotsky called Stalin a bore; Stalin called Trotsky an "actor."

The greatest political issue that divided them was that of "World Revolution" (Trotsky) versus "Socialism in One Country" (Stalin). By 1926 Stalin was directing all the Party's efforts to building socialism within Russia instead of pursuing international class war. Trotsky said this wasn't Marxist, and it would never work. The capitalist nations would unite to destroy the Revolution. Through the years after his exile abroad in 1929 until his murder by an agent of the Soviet secret police in 1940, Trotsky continued to write furious articles against Stalin and his policy.

Luckily for Stalin, Lenin's reliance on Trotsky did not go down well with other members of the Politburo, either. The "Old Bolsheviks" still thought of Trotsky, the ex-Menshevik, as an outsider.

As Lenin's health declined, two Old Bolsheviks, Kamenev and Zinoviev, joined Stalin in secret anti-Trotsky maneuvers in the Politburo. During this crucial period, Trotsky went duck hunting, got his feet wet, and came down with a persistent fever. Both Lenin and Trotsky, the two most powerful members of the Politburo, spent the autumn and winter of 1923 ill in bed, and out of touch.

Stalin, Kamenev, and Zinoviev now mounted an anti-Trotsky public relations campaign. They held meetings without Trotsky, dropping his name "by accident" out of newspaper reports. Insulting speeches against Lenin were dredged up out of

Trotsky's Menshevik past and printed in the papers. "Trotskyism" became the faithless opposite of "Leninism."

Stalin farsightedly made the word "Trotskyism" synonymous with "treason." Everything he did in the blood-soaked years to come was done to protect the revolution of Lenin against the enemy, Trotsky.

LENIN'S DEATH AND "LAST TESTAMENT"

Lenin's death came just in time for Stalin. From his sickbed, Lenin was planning what his secretary called "a bombshell" for Stalin to whom he had once given so much power and responsibility.

In December Lenin's doctors gave strict orders. He must not be upset; he was to have no visitors; he was not to be bothered with affairs of state. And the Central Committee appointed Stalin to see that these orders were carried out. It was allowing the fox to guard the henhouse.

Aware that Lenin's confidence in him was ebbing, Stalin made full use of his guardianship. He did his best to see that Lenin was isolated and not permitted to make government decisions.

One day Lenin dictated to his wife, Krupskaya, a note for Trotsky. Stalin, who had informers even in Lenin's household, heard of it and furiously called Krupskaya. He was in such a state of alarm and rage that he lost control. He shouted and swore at Krupskaya, who complained to Kamenev at the Politburo. "Stalin subjected me to a stream of the coarsest abuse," she wrote. She had never before heard such words from a comrade.[1] That call could have been a bad mistake, for Lenin was not dead yet.

Aware that his days were numbered, Lenin had been composing a *Letter to the Congress*, which became known as "Lenin's Last Testament." It was meant to convey his ideas of how the government should be organized after his death, and it boded ill for Stalin.

In his "testament" Lenin praised and also criticized each member of the Politburo. Trotsky was "distinguished by outstanding ability," but Stalin was a subject for concern. Lenin voiced his doubts that Stalin would use power wisely. He proposed some changes in Party organization to downgrade the bureaucracy that Stalin had been so quietly and carefully building as general secretary. Then Lenin added his "bombshell." "I suggest," he wrote, "that the comrades think about a way to remove Stalin from that position . . ."[2]

When Lenin died in January of 1924, neither Stalin nor the government knew that Lenin was planning to fire Stalin. Stalin, Kamenev, and Zinoviev were already running the country. Trotsky, convalescing by the Black Sea, did not even make it to Lenin's funeral, a serious political mistake. He was later to claim that Stalin & Co. had lied to him about the date of the funeral (although that may have been an excuse for Trotsky's lack of action at such a critical point).

Five months later, when the upcoming Congress of the Soviets was due to meet, Krupskaya brought Lenin's bombshell to the Central Committee. The letter was read aloud to the Committee, which would have to decide whether to put it before the Congress. The scene was intensely embarrassing. Stalin, sitting on the podium under the eyes of the Committee, had to hear himself described as "rude"; he had to listen to Lenin's suggestion that he be replaced with someone "more patient, more loyal, more polite."[3]

But, in fact, the bombshell was more like a damp firecracker. Lenin had criticisms for everyone.

Stalin had Lenin's body embalmed. Hundreds of people have filed by this glass coffin every day. Lenin himself despised the "cult of the individual" and wanted a simple burial.

Trotsky was too far-reaching and self-confident. Kamenev and Zinoviev had dragged their feet at the crucial moment of the November Revolution. Bukharin was "the favorite of the whole Party," but he did not really understand Marxism.[4] No one was eager to have these patronizing slaps on the wrist made public.

Zinoviev came to Stalin's rescue. He said that Stalin had cleaned up his act in the past months, that he had indeed been "patient," "loyal," and so forth, that he was a devout Leninist (unlike that Menshevik, Trotsky), and that above all it was important to preserve Party unity.

This last remark was a telling point. Party unity was sacred. It had made the Revolution, and through the following decades Party members made incredible sacrifices to see that the Party—and with it the Revolution—was safe from divisive influences. Zinoviev suggested that Lenin's letter be suppressed, and it was. Like Lenin and Trotsky, Zinoviev thought Stalin was harmless but useful.

STALIN SETTLES IN

Within two years Zinoviev and Kamenev were running scared. Zinoviev said Stalin was going to ruin the Revolution, and he made a desperate alliance with Trotsky. It was far too late. Stalin promptly allied himself with the other members of the Politburo, Bukharin and Rykov. He already had the Central Committee in his pocket. Now he backed Bukharin's policy of easing up on the peasants. Kamenev and Zinoviev found themselves shouldered out of power.

As soon as that was settled, Stalin changed his tune, and suddenly Bukharin became a "danger to the revolution." As Bukharin said, "He changes his theories depending on whom he wants to get rid of."[5] Bukharin was removed from the Politburo. It all went quite smoothly, with no thought of bloodshed. It was not until ten years later or so that Stalin had all four men shot.

By 1929 Stalin was the sole ruler of Soviet Russia.

CHAPTER 8

HISTORY REVISED

*"Paper will put up with anything
that is written on it."*[1]

—Joseph Stalin

This may be the moment to examine Stalin as a
fabricator of history. While he was in power, and for
long afterward, the truth about Stalin was hard to
come by, and there are still many gaps in the story.

In 1929 Stalin set about to destroy all records of
his past. By that time, he controlled the written
word; everything in print had to pass through the
hands of his censors. He destroyed records, suppressed memoirs, censored historical writings, and
rewrote to his own formula the entire history of the
Bolsheviks before and during the Revolution.

After that Stalin began to silence his old associ-
ates. Some were jailed, and a few were exiled, but
most were executed for unlikely crimes against the
state. These witnesses to history included most of
the original Bolshevik leaders. Many were old comrades who had helped and protected Stalin and
advanced his career in the Party; they included his
own in-laws, his wife's aunts and uncles who had
sheltered him in the old days and had remained

loyal to him in their old age. Few witnesses were left
at liberty to challenge the new history.

All this has made it difficult for historians to trace
the true story of Stalin's youth and the early days of
the Communist party. While Stalin was alive, many
historians relied on his own accounts and on the
official *Big Encyclopedia of the Soviet Union*. But
much of this material was written to glorify Stalin
and cover up the facts. About his family—his two
wives, three children, and parents—Stalin wrote
not a word.

STALIN'S LIFE STORY: PUTTING
THE PUZZLE TOGETHER

More than one historian describes the process of
digging out the facts of Stalin's life as a kind of
archaeology in which every uncovered scrap must
be pieced together with the others to construct a
reasonable picture. The more powerful Stalin became, the more he repainted his self-portrait.

The historian Bertram Wolfe cites a typical example of how Stalin discredited early accounts of the
Revolution. It is the pitiful case of Abel Enukidze.[2]
This Old Bolshevik was, like Stalin, the son of peasants. He had been a friend of Stalin's for thirty years,
sharing the life of the revolutionary. Like Stalin he
had been arrested often anjiaucaped often. He eventually became a well-respected member of the Communist party. Enukidze was one of a very few
comrades to be invited to speak at Stalin's fiftieth
birthday celebration.

But Enukidze also knew that Stalin had actually
played only a small part in the old days. Back in
1903, Enukidze had started to work at an illegal
press, hidden in a subcellar, deep underground in
Baku. For three years he led a secret life in this
basement darkness, turning out issues of *Iskra*, the

party newspaper, as well as copies of *The Commu-nist Manifesto*, revolutionary pamphlets, and pro-paganda. His memoirs describe his life in this dungeon space and the leaders who directed the operation and shared the danger. That press, hidden so skillfully, and used so productively, had a famous and honored place in Bolshevik history. Enukidze had also written many loyal words of praise about Stalin, but unfortunately for Enukidze, Stalin was not mentioned in his memoirs about Baku, simply because Stalin had nothing to do with the Baku press.

On the occasion of Stalin's fiftieth birthday, then, this good old friend was asked to write about Sta-lin's life. Enukidze, ever loyal, did his best to con-nect Stalin with the heroic story of the Baku press. He said that Soso had managed the risky and diffi-cult business of procuring type for the press. It put Stalin in the story, but it was not enough, and it signaled the beginning of the end of Stalin's affec-tion for his old friend.

In 1935 Enukidze was forced to write a long arti-cle for *Pravda*, "confessing" his "errors" in the hum-blest way and increasing Stalin's role in the story. Still not enough. Within a few months Enukidze was denounced as a liar, and finally, in his sixties, this elderly, devoted Bolshevik was executed as a "falsifier of Bolshevik history" and a "mortal enemy of the people." The newest version of the story of the Baku press presented Stalin as the initiator of the whole idea of the hidden press and the director of its activities.

THE GREAT OBSESSION

Why? Why did Stalin care so much about his place in the old stories? Why did he kill people to dress

up his past when his present position was so su-
perbly powerful? If he did not star from the very
beginning, what did it matter? Like everyone else
he'd had to learn the ropes as a young man, and now
his position at the top spoke for itself. Why was
falsifying party history such an obsession? Some
historians take it as evidence that, as Koba, Stalin
had indeed been in the pay of the czar's police; if
that were so, he certainly would have been determined to conceal it.

But this gloomy, angry, pockmarked man seems
also to have had an insatiable need to portray himself as a kind of shining youth, single-handedly carrying the banner of revolution against the foe.
Lenin's friend Nikolai Bukharin said that Stalin
could not bear to feel inferior to another person in
any way, in anything. He certainly took revenge on
anyone who had ever snubbed him as a gauche,
revolutionary nobody.

Last of all, for reasons of vanity and especially for
political purposes, Stalin wanted to portray himself as something we know he was not: Lenin's right-
hand man and natural heir. Lenin was the dominant
figure of the Bolshevik Revolution, and when he
died, Stalin had him preserved—literally. Despite
the furious protests of Lenin's wife, Krupskaya, Stalin had Lenin's body embalmed and put on display
in a glass coffin in a specially built mausoleum in
Red Square. At times the body was touched up and
treated to keep it from decay, and through all the
years that followed—long after the death of Stalin
himself—Russian citizens would file past it weeping and blessing Lenin's name. Only Lenin's portraits were as big as the huge pictures of Stalin that
dominated public squares and buildings in the
years of his dictatorship.

Lenin was a very powerful symbol, and a very

CHAPTER 9

THE WAR AGAINST THE PEASANTS

In December 1929, the country celebrated Stalin's fiftieth birthday. Hysterical with joy, the crowds in Red Square demonstrated that Stalin was now boss (Vozhd) of the Party and therefore the boss of the Soviet Union. A flood of pamphlets and birthday leaflets glorified Stalin as the adored father of the Revolution. People learned that he was the hero of the 1917 Revolution (Lenin was downplayed), that he had led the Red Army to victory (Trotsky wasn't mentioned), that he was the creator and only guardian of Russian Socialism. Thousands of little statues of him appeared like mushrooms overnight. Huge portraits of him stared from every prominent wall. Bureaucrats fawned on him. Schools, towns, factories, were named after him. It was the beginning of the cult of hysterical adoration that was whipped up in the population and lasted until his death.

THE PEASANT PROBLEM

Now that the boss had control of the Party, he had to address an unresolved problem: the problem was

75

that peasants made up 80 percent of the population. The Soviet system from the beginning had been mired in a bog of contradictions. The peasants wanted to be Marxist; that was what the Revolution was all about. But they couldn't. Marx's theories applied to industrial nations, where the workers were the majority. In Russia, however, workers were a tiny minority. Marx supplied no blueprint for bringing the socialist revolution of industrial workers to a country made up of backward peasant farmers.

THE NEP

To complicate matters, a grisly famine had followed the Civil War in 1921. In the Volga region "people ate members of their own families as they died."[1] More than 25 percent of the rural population had starved to death. The famine was caused mainly by the seizure of grain from the peasants to feed the cities.

Revolt and famine had forced Lenin to take a backward step. He had proposed a temporary system that permitted some people to run their own small businesses, left farms in private hands, and allowed farmers on state land to sell their own produce. It was called the New Economic Policy, NEP for short, and it was effective. The economy gradually recovered and so did people's spirits. But the NEP wasn't socialism; it betrayed the ideals of the Revolution. Even the man in the street despised the "Nepmen" who were wheeling and dealing and getting rich in the cities.

The Party leaders wrestled with the problem. None of them could really get comfortable with the NEP, which used the motive of profits to spur the economy; and besides, the peasants had begun to defy the government, refusing to sell grain at fixed low prices.

Everyone—Lenin, Trotsky, virtually all the Old Bolsheviks—agreed that industrialization must be forced, and that the power of the state was needed to force it. The time for the state to "wither away" had not yet arrived. But if Russia must be industrialized, how was it to be done? and how fast? and how should they deal with the peasants?

In 1929, alone in power, Stalin started by getting rid of the NEP. "Either we go backward to capitalism or forward to socialism,"[2] he said. But more than that—he got rid of several million peasants.

How was Russia to industrialize? For more factories you need more workers and more food to feed the workers. For more food you need more modern farms and farm equipment—tractors and harvesters. For more tractors and harvesters you need more factories and factory workers. It was a vicious circle.

Another problem was money; Russia needed foreign credit, money to buy start-up machinery and technology from the West. You could get the money by selling grain to the West. But food, grain, and manpower were all tied up in Russia's little farms, where peasants used wooden plows, and sowed seed and threshed the wheat by hand. They produced barely enough to feed themselves: the "peasant problem" again. No matter what they said to the peasants, Stalin, Lenin, Trotsky, and the others had known from the beginning that the peasants and their 25 million little farms were in the way of the Revolution.

THE FIVE-YEAR PLAN (1929–1934)

Stalin announced a series of steps to build Russian industry, and build it at top speed, by meeting cer-

tain goals every five years. The five-year plan made
Russia the first country in the world to attempt a
planned economy. The plan was directed toward
developing factories, raw materials, and heavy
equipment. First, Stalin set out to deal with the
"problem of the peasants," and the first target was
the peasantry called kulaks.

Kulak means "fist," and kulaks were "the tight-
fisted ones." The name was supposed to describe
peasants who had prospered and who hired other,
poorer peasants to work for them. But, in fact, it
came to mean any peasant who had some farm
animals—a couple of horses, perhaps, or a cow and
some chickens. Any peasant who wasn't dirt-poor
risked being counted as a kulak; and to a peasant
with nothing, anyone with possessions became a
kulak, who could justifiably be robbed.

A few years earlier, in the flush of the New Economic Policy, Nikolai Bukharin (with Stalin's blessing) had cried to the peasants "Enrich yourselves,
develop your farms, do not fear!"[3] Now Stalin announced coolly: "We shall liquidate the kulaks as a
class."[4] It turned out that he meant it literally; hundreds of thousands of peasants were forced off their
farms at gunpoint, deported to labor camps or shot.
Their land, livestock, and equipment were seized to
create collective farms (*kolkhozes*) that would be
more efficient. On the collectives, with vast fields
and specialized equipment, much more grain could
be produced. What is more, one man would theo-
retically be able to do the work of twenty, releasing
labor for the factories.

Aside from its pure inhumanity this policy had
other flaws, and it did not work smoothly. For one
thing, there were still not enough tractors to work
the farms. For another, unskilled peasant labor, sent

to work in factories, produced tractors that broke down almost immediately. For another, few of the peasants on the collective farms were trained in the use and maintenance of machinery, which sat around idle while it rusted to bits.

Stalin's way of smoothing out the bumps was simply to drive faster over them. If the new farms were not producing enough to feed both farms and factory workers, let the farmers eat less. Take more grain from the peasants and feed it to the factories. If there was any left over after that, sell it abroad to earn foreign credit. That peasants would starve was taken for granted. It was necessary, and there were always more peasants.

To help make the system work, the "poor peasants campaign" encouraged the poorest peasants to seize grain and animals from their more prosperous neighbors. Organized groups of city workers and local party activists called "the ten thousands" were employed in the countryside to oversee the seizure of grain, land, and animals from the kulaks.

For the most part, kulaks were not even allowed to join the collectives. "Of course not," Stalin explained; they were the sworn enemies of the collectives. In a kind of irony that became commonplace, the most efficient and hardworking farm families were liquidated. It created an agricultural problem from which the Soviet Union is still trying to recover. But the old agrarian system had to be obliterated; and as for the kulaks, Stalin said "When the head is cut off, why cry about a few hairs?"[5]

Stalin felt that his policies were essential and unavoidable, and he kept himself deliberately from direct experience of the pain they caused. He didn't visit famine areas; he never witnessed the shooting of a peasant family; he never saw the conditions in a labor camp. "One death is a tragedy," he said; "a million is a statistic."[6]

One reason Stalin was in such a hurry to modernize in the 1930s was that he was frantic to catch up with the West. Japan was a threat in the East. Tensions were mounting in Europe. France and England were trying to decide how to handle a new menace rising in Germany—Adolf Hitler. In case of war, Stalin planned to hold off, and if necessary join the winning side. He did not want, he said, "to pull the chestnuts out of the fire" for others.[7] But, for reasons of aggression or defense, he needed to have a military machine: tanks, guns, planes—in a word, industry. "We must not let up," he said. "We are fifty to one hundred years behind the advanced countries. We must catch up in ten years. Either we do it, or they crush us."[8]

After World War II, Winston Churchill asked Stalin if the war had been as bad as the bad times of collectivizing the farms and liquidating the kulaks. "Oh no," Stalin said, "the collective farm policy was a terrible struggle." And it wasn't a question of a few aristocrats, Churchill continued, but millions of small men. "Ten millions," Stalin said, holding up his ten fingers. "It was fearful. Four years it lasted. It was absolutely necessary for Russia."[9]

What the peasant policy did in the end was unleash a famine that dwarfed the great famine of the Civil War. The villagers, pressed to the limit, resorted to their only means of expressing their hatred and despair. They killed their animals and burned their houses and fields rather than hand anything over to the government and the collectives. In just the first few months of collectivization they killed off 15 million cattle and 4 million horses. The wheat fields were turned to blackened burned stubble. And the famine came.

FAMINE ON PURPOSE

There was something different about the famine of 1932–1933, however. Starving the peasants was a deliberate policy, and it was kept a closely guarded secret. No famine relief was requested or allowed. The Soviet newspapers reported nothing, not a word about the famine or the five million or more people starving to death in the Volga area and the Ukraine, once the "breadbasket of Europe." To talk about the famine was a "crime against the state." During the famine, the writer Arthur Koestler traveled through the Ukraine by train and was bewildered by what he saw. "Women were lifting up their infants to the compartment windows—infants pitiful and terrifying with limbs like sticks, puffed bellies, big cadaverous heads lolling on thin necks."[10]

Meanwhile the food that had been taken from the peasants was being exported to earn foreign credit.

THE FIVE-YEAR PLAN IN THE CITIES

The peasants were not the only ones to suffer from the rigors of the first five-year plan. The motto of the plan was: squeeze more out of everybody. In the country it was done by grain "quotas"; in the city "control figures" were used. Factory production requirements were raised and raised again to impossible heights. As workers quit or left for other areas or jobs, new laws were written. You could not leave your assigned job. You could not leave your dwelling place without permission; you could not leave your town without permission and a passport. The government controlled all food supplies, and the threat of going without was used to keep workers in line. The director of a factory had absolute control over the workers, and it was his job to get the work quota out of his people somehow.

Workers were no longer paid by the amount of time they worked, but by the amount they produced (a practice Karl Marx had labeled "exploitation of the worker"). Furthermore, trying to figure out piece rates on, for example, building and repairing individual machines was ridiculous and inefficient. And the pay for this "piecework" kept being lowered. To meet their quotas and to produce enough "pieces" to live, workers abused their machines, ran drills too fast, took no time for oiling or maintenance. Rusting, broken machinery made it harder than ever to keep up with the quotas. The factory director could not afford to sympathize with workers, slaving to do the impossible. If the control figures were not met, the director could be accused of sabotage or treason.

THE LABOR CAMPS

The output of the labor camps was a vital part of the five-year plan, and the campaign against the peasants filled the camps to overflowing. Originally called "corrective labor camps," they were set up in 1917 and their purpose was not to destroy or punish, but to reeducate prisoners and in the process get constructive labor out of them. Prisoners in those days were paid for their labor and were able to support their families and even save a small stake for the time when they were released.

During the 1930s, many of the camps were put under a special department of the secret police (now called the GPU), called Gulag, an acronym for its Russian initials. The laborers in the Gulag camps worked the gold mines of Kolyma in the far east; they built railroads north and east of Lake Baikal and in the far north above the Arctic Circle. They mined coal and built bridges and felled lumber. By 1931 nearly 14 million people filled the camps and millions of them were political prisoners, arrested and deported without trial.

By 1937 the purpose of the camps had expanded. They were not only a source of free labor, they had become a means of killing off prisoners who might be a danger to the regime. Prisoners were made to carry iron railroad ties on their shoulders in summer under the assault of hordes of biting flies; in winter they struggled in thin clothing that got wet and never dried and froze on their bodies. Their food rations were at starvation level and were increased only with increased output. They were worked "*bez-poshchadno,*" "without mercy." Driven to the edge of starvation, eventually they went over the edge. By the end of the 1930s the camps, especially the gold mines, were simply death camps. Above the camps had been written a line from the Soviet Constitution: "In the Soviet Union, labor is a matter of honor, valor, and heroism." By the end of the 1930s the slogan was as ironic as that over Hitler's concentration camps: "*Arbeit macht frei,*" "Work makes man free."

C H A P T E R 10

THE WAY
THINGS WERE

Numbers of people from the West were eager to see the Soviet Union and form their own opinions of it. Many wanted to try their hands at living and working in the Soviet Union.

VISITORS FROM THE WEST

During the 1930s a great economic depression dealt a fearful blow to the nations of Western Europe and to the United States. The jobless rioted in London and Paris. In the United States 10 million people were unemployed. Many Communist party members from these countries went to Russia hoping to find jobs in the factories, mines, and railroads. They were filled with enthusiasm. It seemed a chance at last to help build the Workers' State.

Most of these workers endured a few months or even a year or two, and finally left, dismayed at the lack of food and housing and the maddening inefficiency that put Party functionaries in charge of machines and systems they didn't understand.

An American Communist, who was used to speaking his mind at home, burst out with his criticisms to a factory director: "Why are parts allowed to pile up and clutter up the plant? . . . Why are there so many finished tractors lying about in the open, unused and accumulating rust? Why is it that almost every second worker wears a bandage?"

The director explained: There was no time to repair tractors because malfunctioning ones were being returned to the plant all the time. The workers had to keep up with the quotas.

"Why don't you make fewer tractors and better ones?" he was asked.

"I must follow orders from Moscow," the director explained. "If the Agricultural Department orders more tractors, I must give them what they ask. Orders are orders, and a plan is a plan."[1]

Most of all, the visitors were disheartened and disillusioned when they saw that the Party bureaucrats lived well while workers and peasants had nothing. In Moscow there were special shops for "higher categories" of people: propaganda organizers, military officers, secret police, technicians, engineers, and the like. Workers were not allowed to pass through their doors.

A Soviet military officer described his annual leave in Kursk, where the starving villages had neither food nor fuel. He and other Party officials were housed in a resplendent old czarist palace. Outside it was bitterly cold, and the officer describes how he enjoyed the cozy warmth of the roaring fire:

"Then by some chance I turned suddenly and looked toward the window. I saw the feverish eyes of hungry peasant children—the bezprizornii—their little faces glued like pictures to the cold panes."[2] (Eventually the officer, who continued to be a devout Communist, could stand it no more and defected from the Soviet Union.)

REFORMERS AND WRITERS

A number of distinguished foreign writers visited the Soviet Union in the 1930s, hoping to find a true socialist state. Writers such as Arthur Koestler, André Gide, and Richard Wright came away from Stalin's Russia with sadness and indignation.

Many politicians and economists, however, observing the devastation of the Great Depression, were impressed with the Soviet idea of a planned economy. Indeed, by the time of Stalin's death industrial nations worldwide were trying to develop and plan at least some part of their economies. Today we tend to forget that the Soviets were the first industrial state in history to make the attempt.

Social reformers, diplomats, and reporters from Western countries also wanted to meet Stalin, of course, and they were usually impressed with him. They praised his simplicity (he continued to wear a peasant blouse with pants stuck in his boots in the style of the Caucasus). They felt sympathy for his "natural good manners" (which would have surprised Trotsky, who always criticized Stalin for his foul mouth). Stalin's daughter, Svetlana, said her father could charm anyone when he wanted to make the effort.

The British writer H. G. Wells said, "I have never met a man more candid, fair and honest," to which he added that Stalin's secret strength lay in the fact that "no one is afraid of him and everyone trusts him."[3] U.S. Ambassador Joseph Davies said Stalin was a simple, decent man. The young American writer Lincoln Steffens visited Moscow and talked to Stalin and other Party members. "I have seen the future," he wrote, "and it works!"[4]

THE VALUE OF INCONSISTENCY

Stalin practiced a kind of sleight-of-hand with the Russian people. He changed his tactics and policies whenever it seemed useful to do so. A policy that did not turn out so well suddenly became someone else's idea. (After the war, when Winston Churchill mentioned Stalin's disastrous pact with Hitler, Stalin beckoned to Molotov: "Explain that pact of yours," he said to the embarrassed Molotov.)

Under Stalin nothing was predictable. No one knew what he would do next. It kept people on the defensive and off balance. A party member could be punished today for something he or she was ordered to do a month ago. But when something went sour, Stalin was seldom blamed.

Stalin himself, for example, set in motion the liquidation of the kulaks. By the time the enraged peasants had destroyed tens of millions of farm animals rather than turn them over, and by the time the fields of rusting machinery and poor crops had made it clear that economic disaster was at hand, Stalin published an article with the astonishing title "Dizziness with Success."

The article blamed Party activists for driving the peasants too hard. Why shouldn't a peasant be allowed to keep a cow, or work a garden plot to feed his family? It wasn't necessary to impose such hardship; in fact it was a *mistake*. Local party officials read these words and shivered, while peasants cheered. They thought that Comrade Stalin had at last uncovered the injustice done to them, and they rejoiced.

A few months later, however, the whole thing was reversed. The peasant was back in the *kolkhoz* without his cow, being told by some party hack to plant potatoes where he knew only cabbage would grow—or else he found himself and his family in a cattle car on the way from the warm climates to the frozen arctic and the labor camps.

ART AS PROPAGANDA

Stalin did not neglect the hearts and minds of the people. Russians have always responded with emotion, even passion, to songs and stories. They have never understood why Western governments seem to regard art as something apart from life. The Russian poet Yevgeny Yevtushenko points out that Russian tyrants have always regarded Russian poets as their worst enemies, and Stalin certainly understood that paintings were more than decorations, and that novels and poems were more than entertainments.

The Central Committee voted total state control of these powerful means of expression. Art became social propaganda. The art of the day was called Socialist Realism. It had a message, and the message was the happy Communist worker. Art was to be moral and not "decadent," and music was to be uplifting and inspiring. It showed people a wonderful future—a happy socialist future—as if it were already here. Art became either a political message or an escape instead of a sharper view of reality.

In the movies people were strong and beautiful. There were golden harvests, feasts, and dancing. Stalin himself loved the movies, and his daughter felt that he actually came to believe the propaganda of plenty. Stalin's own table, of course, was plentifully supplied "and he took it for granted," she said, "that art was truthfully reflecting the improvement in living conditions when he saw the same abundance on a movie screen."[5] Perhaps she was naive, but Stalin was indeed very isolated from the everyday life of the Russian people.

The movies proclaimed the Communist ideal, and for the ideal state to come millions of people endured the brutality of the Stalin regime.

SELLING STALIN

The arts were used also for the greatest public relations campaign in history. The Party line had been that the purpose of art should be to further the teachings of Communism, and advance its cause. The Stalinist line was that Stalin's image should be seen in every public building. Every book, newspaper, public meeting, and radio broadcast included and glorified Stalin's name. Writers tried to outdo each other in praise for Stalin, "the genius," "the greatest," "the sublime," and so on.

Yevtushenko recalls that when he was just beginning his career he used to write verses on soccer and volleyball for *Soviet Sport*. The editor, he says, flew into a panic on discovering at the last minute that there was no mention of Stalin in one of the poems. The same thing happened in another publication, and Yevtushenko soon learned the rules: "For a poem to go through there had to be a few lines devoted to Stalin."[6]

Stalin himself edited a groveling, flattering biography that had been written of him. Its every page was crowded with worshipful phrases—"the greatest leader," "the sublime strategist of all times." Stalin is said to have added in his own hand that, although he had led the people with "consummate skill" and was loved by all, he never allowed the "slightest hint of vanity, conceit, or self-adulation."[7] ("Modesty," he told his daughter, "embellishes a Bolshevik."[8])

RUSSIA READS

There were accomplishments as well under Stalin. Thousands of hospitals, child care centers, and schools were built. Stalin sent everyone to school. Before he died, he had raised the literacy rate from rock bottom to a point as high as that of any Western country.

Students were taught to read, but not to think independently. Free inquiry in the sciences was suppressed, and so was free expression in books and newspapers. Children learned by memorizing. They were not taught how to examine a question from different sides, and their lessons did not include question or interpretation of their textbooks. And always included were songs and praises to Stalin and the Party.

One by one, sometimes in batches, the older generation of leaders, with their years of experience outside Russia, was exiled, imprisoned, or liquidated. It was a literate, but semi-educated generation that Stalin raised to face the future.

Marx had suggested religion was dangerous because it taught people to trust in future salvation instead of fighting their oppressors in the present. For Stalin, religion was dangerous because it was the spiritual support and adviser of the peasant. And the church taught the peasant that there was an authority higher than the Party, higher than Stalin— the authority of God.

The "Anti-Religious Five-Year Plan" was announced in 1932. Churches were destroyed or turned into storehouses. Priests were shot in front of

Under Stalin the literacy of the
nation rose dramatically. This is
a schoolroom in Uzbekistan.

their doors, or turned out of their homes and deprived of ration cards for food and of the right to medical care. Their children might survive, but only if they renounced their fathers as traitors, "black crows," and "enemies of the people."

Every government has to give certain people the authority to carry out its programs. These people automatically have prestige, privileges, and power. It is a dangerous fact of life for every large nation. In the Soviet Union, this group, this bureaucracy owed all its privileges to Stalin.

These Party "haves" were determined not to join the "have-nots." If you were a factory manager, a Party official, or an officer of the secret police, you were rewarded with good clothes, good food, a car, a comfortable house or apartment, good schools for your children, and the respect of others like you. You were a member of a privileged class, the very thing the Revolution was supposed to destroy.

But the other side of the coin was fear. Stalin used terror against Party members to keep them from gathering enough power to turn on him. The privileged class were at the mercy of their terrifying leader who could destroy them at a whim—and often did.

To keep Party members in line, Stalin reminded them every so often that what he gave, he could take away. Your wife and children and other relatives would suffer along with you if you failed to meet the approval of the official next in rank above you.

Each head of a department had absolute power over everyone below him: power to hire and fire, to reward and punish, even the power of life and death. In turn he was under the absolute power of his own superior—hopeful of reward, subject to ruin. Responsibility for failure would blow down through the ranks of politicians, Party hacks, soldiers, even the secret police, like a cold wind from Siberia.

Civilian crimes, such as robbery or killing your wife in a fit of rage, were dealt with in an orderly and just fashion. But "crimes against the State," no matter how trivial, carried the threat of death.

"WRECKERS"

To justify harsh programs, the government began to "discover" different conspiracies against the Five Year Plan. A new word came into use—"wreckers." Wreckers were out to sabotage the factories, hide grain, or slow down production. Wreckers were to blame for the hardships. Wreckers were responsible for failed quotas and deadlines. What seemed like a random selection of people would be arrested as wreckers and shot or sent to labor camps. In some cases local Party activists were ordered to "find" a certain number of "wreckers" for the secret police to arrest.

As always, and by design, Stalin kept his personal distance from these activities. They were carried out by the secret police. But according to Nikita Khrushchev, who succeeded as general secretary shortly after Stalin's death, it was Stalin himself who invented the criminal category, "enemy of the people," which made it unnecessary that proof be required before sentence was passed on an accused person.[9]

THE EYES AND EARS OF THE SECRET POLICE

The Cheka, or GPU (soon to be called NKVD), gave Stalin the power to be present at all times in every person's life. The secret police were at everyone's door and window, particularly those of Party leaders. George Orwell's "Big Brother" was no fantasy. He existed in Stalin and his regime.[10]

Schoolchildren were subject to criminal prosecution if they did not report a supper-table conversation in which someone complained about the government or living conditions. To have a serious conversation, friends would "go for a walk," outdoors where they could not be overheard.

Every schoolroom, workshop, art studio, newspaper, store, and office had its GPU informers. You could be accused as a "wrecker" for anything—for a broken tool or a lost identity card. Once accused as an enemy of the people, you had no right to a lawyer or a trial or even to know what you were accused of.

Guilt by association was a powerful weapon. By a law passed in 1932, the family of the accused person was equally guilty and subject to punishment. Great or humble, anyone might be arrested at any time and, it seemed, for any reason. It was all absolutely contrary to the Soviet Constitution, but there was no way for an individual to fight the issue.[11]

Many loyal Communists who worked hard and sacrificed for the Revolution said later that all this seemed like some elemental disaster, like living through a plague. It was just the way things were. It was as if the Revolution had its own strange laws and all one could do was hold on and wait for the better times.

C H A P T E R 11

THE GREAT TERROR

"To purge" means to cleanse, or purify. But in politics, purging has come to mean getting rid of undesirable people. Stalin gave new force to the word. By the middle of the 1930s the purge was synonymous with terror. By 1938, any Party member who had voted in opposition to Stalin since Lenin's death was gone, almost all of them executed. It was a good time to settle scores; a hint would be enough to get a rival or an unlikeable neighbor arrested. The mood of the nation was one of despair and depression. As Stalin's daughter recalls, "People shot themselves fairly often in those days. . . . One leading Party member after another did away with himself."[1]

At the Soviet "Congress of Victors," in 1935, Stalin got a thunderous ovation as he proclaimed the success of the five-year plan and said, "Life has become easier, comrades, more joyous." By the end of the 1930s more than half of the delegates to that congress had been shot. Of the Party Central Committee, 70 percent had been executed.

The purge reached into all levels, not just the Congress and the Central Committee. Heads of committees and departments down the line were purged as "Trotskyites," saboteurs, or "wreckers," to make way for young leaders poured from the new mold. During the purge years from 1931 until World War II, young Communists, workers, and heads of trade unions were called upon to help gather and update personal reports on everyone in the Party. Party members by the thousands were thrown out of their jobs and their apartments; their ration cards were confiscated, their privileges lifted, their civil rights denied.

In 1934 a directive was sent out by Stalin ordering the NKVD to speed up its work. No executions were to be held up; pardons were not to be considered. The NKVD was directed to carry out an execution immediately after a sentence of death was passed.

There had always been cases of real sabotage, of course, from the killing of livestock to the jamming of industrial machines. Much of it was the result of anger and frustration at home. Stalin came to believe that foreign agents were at work inside the Party as well, and that also may have been true. Hitler was coming into power and his sympathizers were being organized into the so-called "fifth column" in foreign countries. Japan was a threat. The Western democracies were anti-Communist. Anyone might be a foreign agent, especially in the mind of Stalin, who grew up breathing the atmosphere of conspiracy.

Another force was at work, too: Stalin's evident feelings of hatred. He hated anyone who "knew too much, or talked too much." Bukharin said, "Stalin knows only vengeance . . . especially on those who are in any way higher or better than he."[2] The Old Bolsheviks—Kamenev, Zinoviev, Bukharin, Trotsky off in exile, and many others—all of them knew that Stalin was neither Lenin nor God and that the Revolution had not fulfilled its ideals.

Stalin now began to get rid of these old war horses, heroes of the Revolution who had known him and taught him and helped him along in his younger, humbler days. He purged them in a strange series of public, circus-like trials—except for Trotsky, who was murdered in Mexico City in 1940. Trotsky was killed on the orders of Stalin, who "could not forget an insult." Stalin might have been thinking of Trotsky when he said, "To choose one's victim, to prepare one's plans minutely, to slake an implacable vengeance, and then to go to bed. . . . There is nothing sweeter in the world."[3]

The Great Terror and the three "show trials" that marked the years from 1934 to 1938 began with a murder. They ended with the disappearance of almost everyone in high places—the top members of the Party, the army, and even the secret police. The Great Terror was Stalin's final push to consolidate his power.

THE KIROV MURDER

The murder that began it all happened in 1934, during a time when everyone was edgy. The unsettling mood had already been established—the feeling that no one was safe from arrest, the knock on the door in the middle of the night. The murdered man was Sergei Kirov, head of the Communist party in Leningrad. The murderer was an obscure, unbalanced young man named Leonid Nikolayev. He had been thrown out of the Party and his motive, he said, was to call attention to the anger felt by the rank and file toward the Party bureaucracy. It is possible, even probable, that the murder was planned by Stalin himself. Kirov was a dangerously popular leader, and he believed in rule by the Party Congress, not by a single person.

Stalin's daughter, Svetlana, was reluctant to believe her father was responsible for Kirov's death. Kirov was a friend of the family, closer to Stalin than his own relatives. She remembers picnics together and how shaken Stalin was when the news came of Kirov's murder. But the evidence is strong that it was engineered for a purpose.

Nikolayev, intent on murder and carrying a pistol, was stopped by guards from entering Kirov's headquarters. He was released on the orders of the Political Police. His pistol was returned to him. When he returned, guards were mysteriously missing, and Kirov walking down the hall was an easy target. Coincidentally, witnesses, guards, and other people involved in the investigation either died "accidentally" or disappeared.

Twenty years later Nikita Khrushchev hinted that Stalin was at the bottom of Kirov's murder. But Khrushchev himself was involved in a power struggle at the time and not everything he said in his famous "secret speech" can be taken as unvarnished truth. In any case, Kirov's murder touched off the years of the Great Terror.

DEATH OF THE OLD
BOLSHEVIKS

In Kirov's murder Stalin discovered more conspiracies "against the people." Nikolayev, he said, was the tool of all kinds of Trotskyist conspiracies and plots against the state. Stalin used the murder of Kirov as an excuse to purge not only Party members who were getting too powerful, but also finally to execute the Old Bolsheviks—men like Rykov, Kamenev, Zinoviev, and Bukharin—who had been on the first Politburo with him. Their executions caused a sensation. The Old Bolsheviks were legendary. To the people they were the heroes of 1917; they had "made the Revolution."

The public was awed. But Stalin knew that men who had mounted one revolution might one day start another. Moreover, we are tempted to guess, Stalin could not stand the fact that they knew he had been neither a hero of the Revolution nor Lenin's chosen heir.

The "show trials" were reported all over the world, and they were accompanied by a bloodbath that robbed the Soviet Union of hundreds of intelligent, experienced managers, professionals, and technicians. The trials were held in Moscow over a period of almost two years. Reporters and foreign diplomats were encouraged to attend. In the course of the trials almost fifty old Party leaders confessed to different acts of conspiracy, to crimes against the state, to treachery of every kind. People who had given their youth to the Revolution, and endured hardship, prison, and Siberian exile, now confessed to plotting with foreign powers, sabotage of the movement, and betrayal of the Soviet Union, as well as plotting the assassination of Stalin.

The three public trials took place in Moscow at intervals during the course of almost two years. They were staged to give maximum publicity to the confessions and to justify the executions. The proceedings were published in the newspapers every day. At the end of each day, the whole transcript of the trial was reported in detail down through every level of the Party organization to the smallest cell, and read aloud at appointed halls, stores, and street corners to an astounded audience.

The Moscow trials stunned Soviet society. It was as if one were to read today that all the justices of the Supreme Court and the president's national advisers along with state governors and heads of Congressional committees were accused of treason, convicted, and executed.

Why wasn't the public suspicious? Many of them were, but anyone high or low who expressed disbelief was arrested as an enemy of the people. One member of Stalin's Politburo described the situation to Khrushchev. A man, he said, might be invited to dinner by Stalin without knowing whether he would go home that night after dinner or find himself under arrest instead.[4]

The show trials still seem fantastic. Why did these people confess in such detail and without accusing their accusers? In 1956 Nikita Khrushchev admitted that torture and blackmail were used to obtain the mysterious confessions. Letters and NKVD files that came to light after Stalin's death, as well as reports from survivors of the purge, confirm the story.

In 1939, says Khrushchev, Stalin sent off a coded telegram to Party and NKVD officials reminding them that the practice of "physical pressure" (a euphemism for torture) was "permissible," "justifiable," "appropriate," and "*obligatory*."[5]

Such techniques as the "conveyer," for example, reduced men of strong character to helplessness without leaving a bruise. In the "conveyer" prisoners were interrogated by teams, working a few hours at a time as on a conveyer belt. The prisoner, however, was not allowed to sleep, lie down, or close his eyes for days on end. Blackmail consisted in terrifying threats against the prisoners' families.

The confessions themselves were elaborate scripts, full of detail, and rehearsed with the accused ahead of time, sometimes over weeks or months, and they always implicated others, who would then confess and implicate still others.

The trials hit the headlines abroad. The Western governments wanted to know the state of affairs in the Soviet Union. They were very uneasy about Adolf Hitler; war seemed inevitable. They wanted to know which way the Soviet Union would jump. Was it strong or weak? Was it riddled with spies? Would it be able to stand up to attack?

United States Ambassador to Moscow Joseph E. Davies went every day to the second trial. He himself was a lawyer, and was keenly interested in the trials from a legal point of view. Were they hoked-up shows to conceal a dictator's power play? Or was there really a conspiracy against the regime? Were the confessions true or false? He was not a sympathizer with the Communist system, and he was expecting to find that the trials were faked. He came away convinced that the accused were guilty and that the trials were conducted properly, according to Soviet law. He said it "would have taken the creative genius of a Shakespeare" to invent and stage the proceedings. He added, however, "The trial was . . . horrible in the impression it made upon my mind. . . ."[6]

One factor, which seems uncommon to the Western mind, was the heroic fervor the Old Bolsheviks attached to the Revolution and the Party. If the unity of the Party could only be saved by these unlikely confessions, then they would make the sacrifice. That argument was in fact used persuasively, and often successfully, by NKVD interrogators.

Outside the high levels of government, many Party members never connected Stalin with what was happening to them. Many victims blamed the judges and the NKVD instead. There were numbers of letters written to Stalin and the Central Committee to "unmask" the NKVD, which was manufacturing evidence and forcing innocent persons to

confess. Many defendants died with praises for Stalin on their lips.

STRIPPING THE ARMY

Sandwiched between the show trials was a secret
trial of the greatest importance. Marshal Tukhachevsky, leader of the Red Army, was accused of
plotting with Germany and Japan to bring down the
Soviet regime. He was shot, and the entire Red Army
was purged as well. This was a closed trial. There
were no confessions, judgment was swift, and the
defendants were executed immediately. All of
35,000 men—half of the officers' corps—were executed. During the first years of Hitler's invasion, the
army operated with inexperienced commanders
and ill-trained troops.

Khrushchev cites false evidence against Tukhachevsky, planted by the Germans, which, he says,
fooled Stalin into executing the cream of his army.
But W. G. Krivitsky, then chief of Soviet military
intelligence in the Hague, says Stalin himself ar-
ranged for the planted evidence to justify his purge.
And we also know that Tukhachevsky was not popular with Stalin. He had seen Stalin bungle a couple
of military campaigns in the Civil War. Stalin might
well have felt that Tukhachevsky, too, "knew too
much."[7]

C H A P T E R 12

STALIN AND HITLER

Stalin had managed, step by step, to take over sole ownership of the USSR. While he was doing it, a new dictator was rising in Europe.

Adolf Hitler began his career in the 1920s, and the West watched, at first unconcerned and then with alarm, as his influence in Germany grew. By 1933 he was an important threat.

If the West was afraid of Hitler and war, so was Stalin. He recognized in Hitler a man equally determined and ruthless. Hitler's announced program to dominate the world and his rage against Communists and Jews seemed to be the ravings of a madman.

But Stalin recognized Hitler's implacable force. He knew that war would come, and he was determined not to enter on the losing side. During the first year after Hitler became chancellor of Germany, Stalin kept a low profile; he kept perfectly quiet, watching and waiting as he had done so often before when important choices were to be made.

Isolation was Stalin's nightmare. His troops were involved in clashes with Japan, which threatened Russia's borders to the east. Hitler's forces loomed to the west. The capitalist democracies would not risk themselves to help protect Russia from Hitler. Britain was doing everything to avoid war, and it seemed possible that she might conclude a separate peace with Germany. In the West only Poland stood between Stalin and Hitler.

CONFUSING FOREIGN POLICY

During those years no nation's foreign policy was clear, and Stalin's foreign policy took so many twists and turns that it baffled even the Communists, especially Communists abroad.

The Communist International, the Comintern, set up by Lenin, was an association of Communist movements throughout the world. Its aim was worldwide socialist revolution and members took their cue from the Soviet Union. Now Comintern members couldn't keep track of the shifting line. They were told to fight fascism one day and to cooperate with Hitler the next. They were told to cooperate with social democrats in Western governments, whereas they were strictly forbidden to do so before, as these governments were considered capitalist tools. But world revolution was not Stalin's great priority, and what he wanted now was protection for the Soviet Union.

The greatest danger for Stalin lay in the fact that the Soviet Union was not ready for war. Despite all the rejoicing at the Congress of Victors, the country's industry was not productive enough for war. The most experienced generals and officers of the army had been shot. The best brains of the Party had been shot, too. Stalin needed to play for time.

THE TEAMS LINE UP

At this point all the nations that would be on stage for the Second World War were worried about who would be on which side. Hitler was building a monstrous war machine with the frenzied approval of thousands of Germans who suffered from desperate unemployment and national shame for their defeat in the First World War. Hitler blamed all their problems on the Western powers, the Jews, and the Communists.

The future Allies—Britain, France, the United States, and the Soviet Union—all saw war coming, but no one wanted to wage it. Britain and the United States were careful to avoid new military alliances or promises that would draw them into war.

Stalin spun around like a top. He sent out feelers to the West. He established formal relations with the United States. He joined the League of Nations (which Lenin had called a "robbers' den" of colonial powers). In the Spanish civil war, he supported the Loyalists against the Fascists. He approached Britain and France, probing for guarantees of collective security. Playing both ends against the middle, Stalin negotiated secretly at the same time with Hitler, who turned him down—temporarily.

PACTS WITH HITLER

In 1938, when Hitler was ready, he annexed Austria and laid claim to part of Czechoslovakia. Britain and France, desperately hoping to avoid war, signed the Munich Pact with Germany, giving Hitler what he wanted. Hitler marched into Czechoslovakia; Poland was to be next. With his plans made for Poland, Hitler now saw an advantage in a nonaggression pact with the Soviet Union.

On August 23, 1939, the Soviet Union signed the pact with Germany. The pact included a secret agreement to recognize Russian and German spheres of influence in eastern Europe. It gave Russia a free hand in the Baltics, which had been part of czarist Russia, and a large slice of Poland. Now Russia would have a buffer on her western flank.

The pact with Hitler stunned the Russian people and Communists everywhere. Germany had always been their natural enemy. Hitler had proclaimed his hatred for Communism and vowed death to the Communist "red rats." But now Communists were told to abandon the anti-Nazi posture. In the Soviet Union anti-Nazi slogans, posters, books, and movies disappeared.

Insofar as it was a political agreement, the pact shamed Communists at home and abroad. However, the Russian people, hungry and desperately tired, could and did understand the need for a military agreement that might keep them out of war. Stalin abandoned Communist theory for the practical need to deflect Hitler's machine from his borders.

Within days of signing the pact with Russia, Hitler marched into Poland. It was blitzkrieg, "lightning war," a blast without warning. German planes flew over Poland and the bombing and strafing began; Britain and France finally declared war on Germany. World War II began on September 3, 1939.

In accordance with his secret agreement with Hitler, Stalin invaded Poland from the East. He took the eastern area, whose main population was ethnically Ukrainian rather than Polish.

Stalin hoped to unite this Ukrainian population with the Soviet Ukraine. He wanted people there who would accept without fuss a separation from the rest of Poland. For this, he needed to get rid of as many ethnic Poles as possible. He did it with mass arrests and the deportation of millions of Poles to the labor camps, where they were put to work and driven savagely as Stalin raced against time to complete his modernization of Russian industry.

THE STORY OF KATYN

When Stalin took "his share" of Poland, many Polish soldiers and officers were sent to Russian prison camps. The peculiar fortunes of war found the Poles becoming the uneasy allies of the USSR against Germany after 1941. A Polish government-in-exile was established in London. At Churchill's urging, many Poles in Russia were freed, and Poles began to organize a new army on Russian soil, under Soviet authority, to help fight Hitler. The soldiers and officers in the prison camps, some 15,000 of them, were to be released to form the Polish units.

But they were nowhere to be found. The prisoners were traced to three Russian camps where they had been held until the previous year, 1940. Both NKVD records and Polish military records were very complete. It was known to a man who had been taken prisoner by the Russians. But now the prisoners had disappeared.

The Polish diplomats in Moscow made inquiries. Moscow was vague. No one knew where the Polish officers were. Stalin said they must have been released, or perhaps they had fled to Manchuria or somewhere. "Those men," said the Polish general, "those men are *here*." Not one of them had come back from the camps.[1]

Early in 1943 the Germans who now occupied Smolensk announced that they had found mass graves in the forest of Katyn near Smolensk. The missing Polish officers, thousands of them, had been shot through the base of the skull and buried under the forest floor. Who had done it? The men had been shot with German bullets, but the Germans said the NKVD had murdered them, using captured ammunition as a cover-up.

American newspapers reported the "Mystery at Katyn." The Americans and the British (particularly Churchill) suspected that the Germans were correct; the officers had been missing since 1940, when the Germans had not yet advanced to Smolensk. But Churchill would not respond to the indignant Polish government-in-exile, which believed the NKVD was guilty. The Poles demanded an investigation.

Churchill bluntly turned them down. He had a war to win, and the Allies needed Stalin. Furthermore, Stalin was an ally whose soldiers and people were fighting the war in Europe virtually alone; the Allies had still not invaded Europe to relieve Hitler's relentless pressure on the Soviets.

A BLUNDER BECOMES AN ADVANTAGE

The argument over who was responsible for the tragedy at Katyn became one basis for Stalin's later control of Poland. He flatly denied any Russian involvement in the massacre, which was indeed handled in typically Nazi style. He now had a good excuse to accuse the Polish government-in-exile of being unfriendly.

Stalin fostered a group of Polish patriots in Moscow—patriots, but men who would not raise an argument over the chunks of Poland he had bitten off in 1939. It was the nucleus of an alternative Polish government, friendly to Stalin. When the war was winding down, Stalin's allies could not refuse him the right to insist on "friendly" governments on

Corpses of the missing Polish soldiers are uncovered in this mass grave in the forest of Katyn.

his borders, and there was no doubt that the Poles in Moscow were "friendly," and the Poles in London were not.

Stalin manipulated the situation and the people involved with great skill; Churchill and Roosevelt were to learn more of his talents two years later at the Big Three Conferences at Teheran and Yalta. Stalin got to keep his slice of Poland, and Poland became a satellite of the Soviet Union.

Years after the war, when the Soviet Union was beginning to reject Stalinism, the records and facts were revealed that proved that the Katyn massacre was indeed the doing of the NKVD.

CHAPTER 13

WORLD WAR II

All the great powers opposed to Hitler made mistakes in the years leading up to World War II. The United States tried to isolate itself from the problem of Hitler. Britain tried to appease Hitler with a mouthful of Czechoslovakia. France relied on the protection of her Maginot Line, a series of underground forts along the border with Germany. And Stalin thought his pact with Hitler could hold off the German menace and allow the Soviet Union to enlarge its frontiers at the same time—while France and Britain did the work of containing Hitler. As it happened, it was Stalin who would have to contain Hitler, and his country would pay a terrible price.

After concluding his pact with Hitler, Stalin occupied Estonia, Latvia, and Lithuania—old possessions of czarist Russia. Then he entered into an embarrassing war with Finland, also part of the czar's old empire, but Finland held the Russian Bear at bay longer than anyone thought possible. World opinion was shocked. Russia was thrown out of the League of Nations, and Stalin found himself more isolated than ever. In addition, the war with Finland demonstrated what the future allies feared and what Hitler hoped: the Russian army was weak, ill-supplied, disorganized, and stripped of its top officers and most of its officer corps.

Hitler's speed and success startled Stalin, who had hoped to win time while Hitler fought his way across Europe. By late 1940 Hitler had gobbled up Denmark in a day, Norway in a matter of weeks. Holland, Belgium, then France fell. By the spring of 1941 Hitler was the master of Europe. His invasion machine seemed invincible.

STALIN PANICS

Stalin was afraid. Khrushchev said Stalin was "paralyzed by his fear of Hitler, like a rabbit in front of a boa-constrictor."[1] If Hitler came against Russia, all that Stalin had done—dragging Russia out of its dark peasant background with terror, blood, and blackmail—would be for nothing. His power would be snatched from him; he himself would face death or imprisonment or worse. And Russia would become the serf of Germany.

The last may have been as important as the first. Stalin may have been obsessed with power, but he was also obsessed with his vision of Russia. It should be remembered that in the beginning no Marxist considered it possible to have a workers' revolution in a country of backward farmers. Stalin, using brute force, had carried out a kind of reconstructive surgery that broke the very bones of his huge nation and remodeled it beyond recognition. Modern Russia was his creation.

In 1941 both Stalin's power and his nation lay seemingly helpless under the shadow of Hitler's descending boot. Stalin absolutely refused to face the truth. The intelligence services of Britain and the United States, as well as Stalin's own spies in Germany, knew what was coming. They tried to warn Stalin. His own generals warned him. German troops were massing at the border. Even the day of the planned German invasion was known—June 22.

But Stalin rejected every warning. His common sense deserted him, and no one in Russia had the authority to move without him. He seemed paralyzed with fear. For over a week he refused to mobilize the army, for fear of provoking Hitler.

He had killed off the experienced officers of his own army. Now he would not even give the orders for the troops to defend themselves. While Hitler's armies assembled at the Soviet frontier and his planes made reconnaissance flights over Soviet soil, Stalin's citizens were reading about sports on the front pages of *Pravda*.

THE INVASION OF RUSSIA

Hitler attacked at dawn on June 22, 1941, the anniversary of Napoleon's invasion of Russia over a century earlier. Stalin's soldiers scattered before the Nazi advance. Stalin still could not take it in. He convinced himself that Hitler was playing a deep game, trying to get Stalin to attack the German army and break the pact. Even after the German offensive began, Soviet artillery commanders were ordered to hold their fire. The generals and the Politburo were desperate to get Stalin to act. The Central Committee was summoned to Moscow, but Stalin refused to see them.

At the front, thousands of Soviet soldiers were killed or taken prisoner. In a little over two weeks

The couple has discovered the body
of their son, executed by the Nazis.

Hitler advanced 300 miles, picking up equipment abandoned by the fleeing soldiers. Statues of Stalin were toppled and his huge portraits were ripped from walls and buildings. Stalin himself did not speak to the Russian people for over a week. Some say he went into a deep depression and hid out in his country house near Moscow, unable to rouse himself to act. Others say he simply went on a monumental drinking spree in the Kremlin. Whatever the reason, while he wrestled with himself the German forces rolled east, headed for Moscow, Stalingrad, and Leningrad.

Stalin's panic was unbelievably costly in lives, land, and weapons, but it did not last for long. By July 3 he was more or less in command of himself; by early August he had assumed supreme command of the army. Eleven days after the invasion he finally summoned up the nerve to talk to the people. It was a huge relief to the country, even though the news was bad. At least the leader was back at his post.

In a stifled, hoarse voice, sighing frequently, Stalin addressed the people as "Comrades," "citizens," "dear friends, brothers and sisters."[2] He appealed to them to fight against enslavement by Hitler's "fiends." More characteristic was his notice that whiners, cowards, and deserters would be dealt with harshly (shot).

SCORCHED EARTH

Then Stalin called for a policy of "scorched earth." Whenever they were forced to retreat, the people were to leave a desert behind them. "The enemy must not have a single engine, a single railroad car, a pound of grain or a gallon of fuel. . . ." He told them to "blow up bridges and roads, tear down telephone

lines, set fire to forests, stores, transportation. . . .
Conditions must be made unbearable for the enemy. . . ."[3]

The German army now advanced through a
wasteland of burning fields, broken bridges,
wrecked houses mined with booby traps. It was a
terrible and awe-inspiring action. People burned
their houses and possessions, torched their farms,
blew up and reduced to one vast, burning dump all
the places they had loved.

Before November the Germans had killed or
wounded 2 million Russians and taken 2 million
more as prisoners. They were in possession of more
than half of Russia's iron, coal, and steel production;
over one third of its grain; and over 40 percent of its
railroads. By December, German forces were nearly
in sight of the Kremlin's towers.

Morale was an urgent concern. The rifles of the
NKVD at their backs could force the soldiers to fight,
but it could not call up enthusiasm or heroism.
Only fierce determination and morale could keep
the terrified and exhausted people from giving up
the struggle.

SAVE THE FATHERLAND

Stalin had cowed the people with terror. Now he
appealed to their patriotism. He knew that a call to
defend the fatherland would appeal to a much wider
base than a call to defend socialism and the Party.

In doing so Stalin broke every Marxist law. Western minds are brought up on the idea of national
loyalty—"I only regret that I have but one life to lose
for my country"; "My country right or wrong." But
Marx had taught that nationalism just protected
capitalist governments that oppressed the workers.

Lenin had taught loyalty to the Party, not to the nation. Patriotism was something the Bolsheviks had wanted to suppress. Now Stalin called upon it in Russia's darkest hour.

The response was powerful, for the love of Russia was deep and strong in the population and in Stalin himself. The vast majority of the people had been peasants, physically and almost mystically bound to the land they tilled. As for the workers, whose numbers had so greatly increased with the surge of new industry, they took enormous pride in their achievement and in their country. It was, after all, the only country in the world to have achieved a socialist revolution. The more isolated the nation became, the more strongly the people drew together.

A CALL TO ARMS

In the autumn of 1941, with the German army approaching, the traditional military parade was held in Moscow on the anniversary of the Revolution. There was heavy cloud cover that gave protection from Hitler's warplanes. Stalin stood on Lenin's tomb and addressed the people in that low, slow, cold voice.

He appealed to the people's love of Russia and her long, enduring history. He reminded them of the great fighters of the imperial past. He invoked their hatred of the invaders who were dealing out incredible atrocities in the occupied lands. He ended with a call to arms whose predictable drama contrasted strangely with his flat, emotionless voice: "Death to the German invaders. Long live our glorious fatherland, its liberty, its independence. Under the banner of Lenin, forward to victory." It was not great speechmaking, but it was a message his people wanted to hear and they cheered him under the cloud cover that held off the planes of Hitler's *Wehrmacht.*

HITLER'S BLUNDER

With the Germans almost at the gates of Moscow, the people were terrified. The Soviet government was moved out of the Kremlin and far to the east. To the people of the city, it was like an admission that the war had been lost. They began to burn their Party cards. Soldiers put on civilian clothes. Hysterical crowds dashed here and there preparing to flee the city.

Stalin, who had panicked in June, now stayed in Moscow, facing Hitler's armored columns. That simple fact rallied the people more than anything else in those desperate days, and they never forgot it. As the German army advanced, the news was passed around that Stalin was there, at his post in the Kremlin. There could not have been a more powerful booster for Russian morale.

In the battle for Moscow, it was not Stalin's strategy, but Hitler's blunder that saved the city. As Stalin reminded his people, the deeper Hitler penetrated Russia, the longer and less secure his supply lines would be. When Hitler postponed the campaign for the winter, leaving his troops encamped outside Moscow, he made a fatal mistake. His soldiers did not even have winter-weight uniforms.

In one of the worst winters on record, Hitler's battalions hunkered down outside Moscow in hostile, unfamiliar countryside, with no fuel, no warm clothes, no proper shelter. More German soldiers died from the cold that winter than from Russian bullets. The German army was forced into its first military retreat since Hitler's rise to power.

SUPREME COMMANDER-IN-CHIEF

Stalin took command of all the military forces. He drove himself and everyone around him. He was in personal charge of every important department, from supplies to the movements of troops, the tactics and the strategy. His orders were to be obeyed quickly, and there was no such word as impossible. As a result, sometimes the impossible was accomplished.

At other times Stalin's demands seemed based on a fantasy that anything was possible if he commanded it. Retreat was forbidden. Stalin's generals often found that any decision made without Stalin could end a general's career, and possibly his life. Army movements were held up waiting for communication from Moscow, and then both the people and the Red Army suffered unnecessary and expensive losses.

Churchill, however, admired Stalin's grasp of strategy. Explaining new and unorthodox plans to Stalin, he said "I never saw a man grasp a difficult problem so quickly. He had it in a flash."⁴ Stalin seems to have been good at the big picture, but not the day-to-day battle. He seldom understood that tactical retreat could save men and weapons to fight another day.

People argue to this day about Stalin as a war leader. But most agree that throughout the war he alone was in charge, and not one important military action was taken without his say-so.

"UNCLE JOE"

While Soviet soldiers and civilians battled against the undivided forces of the German army, the Allied governments kept putting off the invasion of Europe. They were worried about having sufficient landing craft and shipping. (There is also some argument that at first the Allied governments were not against letting Stalin weaken himself while he kept Hitler pinned down.)

The people in America and England, however, were full of admiration and sympathy for Russia and "Uncle Joe," who was fighting the war so gallantly and so alone. The long delay in mounting the second front may have been necessary, but it cost Russia thousands of lives and the terrible destruction of cities and countryside. Stalin did not let the West forget it when the Big Three met at the bargaining tables toward the end of the war.

Within Russia, too, Stalin was largely revered. Throughout the war he was extremely popular among the citizens of the Russian republic.

THE NKVD: STILL AT WORK

But many among the national minorities were not willing to die for Stalin, or for Russia. Thousands of Cossacks joined Hitler's armies. Ukrainians, who had suffered when Stalin so brutally collectivized the farms, greeted the Germans as liberators. In the Baltics, too, many people waited eagerly to be "liberated" by Hitler.

The NKVD slaughtered people by the thousands as the German armies advanced, and again as the Germans retreated. As the Germans approached, the NKVD mowed down prisoners in Soviet jails and labor camps. Then, as the Soviet army moved back through lands that the Germans had occupied, the NKVD gathered up minorities, and "unreliables" contaminated by contact with the Germans.

They arrested many Poles, Rumanians, Baltic peoples, Ukrainians—anyone who might be considered as a possible opponent of the Communist Party regime. These people were taken by the thousands and sent to build the roads, fell the forests, and mine the ore of Siberia.

Whole villages of self-governing minorities were deported, not to labor camps, but to remote regions in Siberia and Asia. Of them, Stalin had written in his book *Marxism and the National Question* (1913) that they would be treated as free and independent peoples in the newly organized state, with the right to secede if they wanted to. Now the Karachis and Kalmyks, the Chechens and Ingusi, the Balkars, the Crimean Tatars, were uprooted and deported. Their autonomous regions were dissolved and the populations were sent far from home.

DEATH TO SPIES

Lapses in army morale were punished by a division of the NKVD called Smersh. Smersh is short for *smert shpionam*, "death to spies." One of its functions was to ride herd on the army. Officers or their soldiers who did not show sufficient ardor in battle were shot on the spot. Soldiers were ordered to die rather than be taken by the enemy. Surrender was treason, and anyone taken prisoner was considered to have surrendered voluntarily.

Stalin's son Yakov, the son of his first wife whom he loved so much, was taken prisoner by the Germans. By some accounts the Germans offered to trade him for a captured German general, but Stalin refused. Stalin's daughter says that her father told a foreign correspondent that there were no Russian prisoners in Germany, only Russian traitors whom the government would "deal with" after the war. Asked about Yakov, Stalin said "I have no son called Yakov."[5]

Stalin's older son Yakov died in a German concentration camp, possibly a suicide. (Right) Yakov with Nazi officers; (below) Yakov's body rests against barbed wire.

Yakov later died in a German concentration camp. Yakov's wife was taken from her small daughter and sent to prison for two years under another law that was passed to punish families of prisoners of war.

The Germans themselves gave people a strong incentive to fight. Those who surrendered to the Nazi forces found the Nazis far worse than the NKVD. Prisoners became slave labor—if they were lucky. Slavs and Jews were considered inferior by the Nazis. Old men and women, children, and infants were burned or shot. Many were tortured before they were killed.

STALINGRAD AND LENINGRAD

The people of the Soviet Union became convinced that Stalin alone could save them, and he in turn gave them confidence that Hitler could be beaten. At the battle of Moscow, he reminded them, had they not been the first people ever to turn back the German war machine?

Now, "fighting like wild animals" the Russians turned the Germans back at Stalingrad—but not without horrible sacrifice. Stalingrad was in a useful strategic position on the Volga but it was also a symbol both to Hitler and to Stalin. (The Soviet government has since renamed the city Volgograd, but back then it bore Stalin's name.) Stalin was determined to hold the city, but his strategy was pitiless to his own people. The Germans bombed Stalingrad almost to rubble before their troops entered the city, but the soldiers and the people of Stalingrad were ordered to hold out.

And they did hold out. Week after week, day after day, for almost seven months, they fought from house to ruined house, street by street, while Marshal Zhukov assembled and positioned the forces with which to trap the German army.

In November Zhukov struck; first with bombard-ment, then with tanks, then with infantry. Under siege, the German soldiers froze through the winter in the city. By February it was all over. The trapped German forces surrendered. Stalingrad was the be-ginning of the end for Hitler. With the battle of Kursk in July and August of 1943, the German army went on the defensive and the Red Army became the attacker.

THE 900 DAYS

During all this time, from November 1941 until the end of January 1944, Leningrad was under siege. The siege of Leningrad has a special and terrible place in history. Bombed and cut off from supplies, Leningrad starved and froze and resisted for 900 days, two and one-half *years*. There were three mil-lion people in Leningrad when the siege began. Nearly half of them died.

Most of them died in the winter of 1941–42 when the temperature fell 10, 20, 30 degrees below zero, while the bombs and artillery shells fell and there was no food, no water, no light, no heat. By then the people ate library paste; they ate their dogs; eventu-ally they ate their dead. Trenches were dynamited in the frozen ground for mass burials, but every day the piles of corpses grew higher. Along the roads to the cemeteries and behind the hospitals, bodies were stacked like cordwood. The corpses were transported, like everything else, on children's sleds, the only transportation left. People sat down and died in the streets, their faces black and shrunken.[6]

Stalin's refusal to believe in the German attack

had allowed the German army to advance on Leningrad by September 1941. Three years after the war, Stalin had almost every official who had been involved in the heroic defense of the city shot. They were charged with treason and conspiracy to turn the city over to the Germans.

After Stalin's death and the opening of secret military records, policies and blunders that prolonged the siege were revealed.

THE BIG THREE

The war had drawn together three leaders so unlike in background and beliefs that agreement between them seemed impossible. The American president, Franklin D. Roosevelt—wealthy, educated, democratic, and informal—was full of American optimism. British Prime Minister Winston Churchill, the aristocrat, had been born to the traditions of empire—the pride, advantage, and responsibility of ruling others. And then there was Stalin, the peasant, trusting no one, an Old Bolshevik bred on conspiracy, hating the West, and committed to the idea of a workers' socialist state.

Two of these "Big Three" were responsible to elected governments. There were many decisions, even in the crisis of war, that they could not make alone. Stalin had to get used to hearing them say, "My Congress won't stand for that," or "I will have to put that before my government." Stalin alone was the absolute boss in his country, responsible to no one, able to make any decision at any moment, as he wished.

The Big Three shared only two things: to start with, fear of Hitler; in the end, victory over him. Then they separated. Their abiding differences divided them even before the end of the war. Roose-

The Big Three at Teheran:
Stalin, Roosevelt, Churchill.

velt, who once told Churchill, "I think I can handle Stalin,"[7] ended by confessing to his advisers, "I can't tell a good Russian from a bad one," and admitted that Stalin baffled him.[8]

By November of 1943 the Big Three knew they were winning the war. They met at Teheran in Iran to decide their strategy for finishing Hitler off, and they met in 1945 at Yalta on the Black Sea to map out the future for postwar Europe. At Teheran, they agreed to prepare for the long-awaited Operation Overlord, the invasion of France by the combined British and American forces. At Yalta it became clear to all that the Soviet Union was not going to back away from territories it had occupied during the war.

The Soviets had suffered many more losses than all their allies together—seventy-five times more than the United States; forty-two times more than Great Britain;[9] more than any nation in history. When Stalin insisted that there should be "friendly" governments on his borders, no one could find it unreasonable. At the end of the war Russia retained possession of the Baltic states and the eastern half of Poland (which got East Prussia for compensation). Communist governments, christened "peoples' democracies," took over in occupied Poland, Czechoslovakia, Hungary, Rumania, Bulgaria, Yugoslavia, and East Germany.

They were independent Communist governments at first. Except for Yugoslavia they soon became "puppet" governments of the Soviet Union, tied to the Soviet economy, sealed off from Europe, and united in an Eastern Bloc confronting the West.

CHAPTER 14

THE COLD WAR

After the war, for a brief moment, a new openness between Russia and the West seemed possible. Before the war's end Stalin himself had spoken for peaceful coexistence between Russia and the West.

Stalin now had the protection of friendly Communist governments on his European borders. Eastern Europe was out from under the heel of Hitler, and states such as Rumania were also out from under creaking, encrusted feudal regimes that had ruled them before the war. People in the streets of Rumania welcomed Soviet soldiers with kisses and tears of joy, just as Americans were greeted at the liberation of Paris.

The new Communist governments in eastern Europe had great success at first. The old regimes were swept away; land was given to the peasants; the working class was given control of the factories. And in the Soviet Union people looked forward hopefully to a life of peace and relief from fear and hardship. But it was not to be.

The Cold War was a state of political tension and mutual fear and loathing that kept East and West divided and threatened by war clouds for more than a decade. Stalin, an old man now, was determined that any future war would not be fought on Russian soil; the vulnerable open plains of Russia had been invaded too often before. And Stalin felt besieged, by enemies from within and by anti-Communist governments outside. The United States in particular was more fully industrialized, and had more powerful military weapons, including the atomic bomb. To Stalin, the West spelled nothing but danger.

The Cold War was also fueled by the West, fearful of Soviet expansion. Stalin had hoped for a loan from the United States and large reparations from Germany, but, as the Allies reminded him, severe reparations against Germany after World War I had not served the cause of peace. They would not agree to strip Germany completely. And the new United States president, Harry Truman, did not come through with the hoped-for loan.

It was obvious to Stalin that the West wanted to secure as much of Europe as possible from falling into his "sphere of influence." On his side, Stalin was just as determined to control absolutely the Soviet-occupied nations on his European borders. He needed them both for economy and for defense. He needed their industry and their trade, and he wanted them tied to the Soviet Union, not wheeling and dealing with Western markets and governments.

NATIONS BECOME SATELLITES

But Stalin had never been able to support the idea of Communist nations independent of Russia. Communist China alarmed him; independent Yugoslavia enraged him. Stalin was determined to graft the peoples' democracies to the flanks of the Soviet Union.

Again, the ax fell most heavily on the Communist party itself. In Czechoslovakia, Hungary, Rumania, and Bulgaria the Party was purged with the help of the NKVD. The prisons were filled as Stalin-style show trials were staged, complete with "confessions." Stalinists replaced the independent Communists, and the peoples' democracies became satellites of the Soviet Union.

GOING HOME

Stalin dealt just as harshly with returning citizens who had been in the West, even those who had seen the West from behind the barbed wire of a German concentration camp. At the Yalta conference, the Allies had agreed to send back to the Soviet Union, by force if necessary, all Soviet citizens who had left the USSR before and during the war. It was a cold-blooded decision, one the Allies had agreed to because they still depended on Stalin to carry on the war against Germany.

Now, almost everyone who had emigrated was sent back to Stalin. It was not entirely unexpected that people such as Cossacks who had actually collaborated with the Germans would be dealt with as traitors; but according to Soviet law, their wives and children were equally guilty. Many people, sometimes whole families, committed suicide rather than face the prospect of going home. Families fell on their knees pleading with Allied troops not to send them back, but soldiers grimly, some in tears, obeyed orders and forced them onto the trains headed east.

Prisoners of war, who had been held in German concentration camps, suffered the same fate. Official documents were read to them promising that they would be welcomed at home. Once on Soviet soil, however, some were tried in groups and swiftly executed; others were sent to replenish the supply of labor in the 165 or so groups of Soviet labor camps. (Did they remember Stalin's saying that there were no Russian prisoners of war, only Russian traitors that he would "deal with" after the war?)

In Stalin's eyes, or in the eyes of the NKVD, officials and soldiers who had been attached to embassies or regiments abroad were also contaminated from contact with the outside world. They were sent to special camps for "re-education."

Altogether, the Allies sent back to Russia over 2 million souls. More than half of them were convicted of treason as soon as they reached Soviet soil. (It was not until years later that the United States began to accept and protect "defectors" who fled to the West.)

NO TOASTERS; MORE STEEL

In late 1946, Stalin, more concerned than ever with building a fortress against the West, announced to his people not relaxation and an easier life, but a new series of five-year plans to develop more heavy industry. That meant that consumer goods, the things that ease the day-to-day lives of people—clothes, housing, cars, appliances—came least and last. The government scornfully called it "cotton-dress production."

A rise in steel, coal, and oil production of up to 500 percent was demanded. The manufacture of railroads, trucks, planes, and armaments was once more stepped up. The sciences of physics and mathematics were the only ones Stalin didn't meddle with, except to urge them on toward the development of a Russian atomic bomb.

To keep his people from demanding a higher standard of living, Stalin had to shield them from knowledge of life in the West. Stalin began to re-educate his people to despise their one-time allies. Russians had grown positively fond of the West during the war. When President Roosevelt died in America, people wept for him from Moscow to Minsk. Now Stalin gave the people a booster inoculation against the West.

Cartoons showed Churchill as a drooling old man with grasping fingers being held at bay by a stern, young, Soviet soldier. Uncle Sam appeared as a greedy warmonger clutching fistfuls of blood money. New laws made it a criminal act to praise the United States. Marriages to foreigners were forbidden. The people were informed that Russia alone had won the war. The government began a ludicrous campaign to prove that every modern technical advance—from electricity to the airplane—had come from Russia.

THE IRON CURTAIN FALLS

Stalin turned his back on the West, pulled the doors closed behind him, and locked them with a heavy key. All contact with the West was severed. In 1946 Winston Churchill, speaking to an American audience, said "From Stettin in the Baltic to Trieste in the Adriatic an iron curtain has descended across the Continent."[1] (See map on facing page.)

The West, in alarm, went anti-Communist. People were really reacting mostly against Stalinism, but by now Stalin and Communism seemed like the

ATLANTIC
OCEAN

SWEDEN

FINLAND

NORWAY

Leningrad

BALTIC
SEA

NORTH
SEA

ESTONIA

LATVIA

SOVIET
UNION

DENMARK

LITHUANIA

Berlin

POLAND

EAST
GERMANY

WEST
GERMANY

CZECH.

AUSTRIA

HUNGARY

ITALY

RUMANIA

YUGOSLAVIA

BLACK SEA

BULGARIA

ALBANIA

TURKEY

GREECE

MEDITERRANEAN SEA

The Expansion of the Soviet Union
in Europe During World War II

Occupied by the
U.S.S.R 1939-46

Annexed by the U.S.S.R.
from Germany and
Czechoslavakia

Soviet satellite states of
Eastern Europe. (Yugo-
slavia broke with the
U.S.S.R. in 1948.)

Iron Curtain

same thing. United States Secretary of State James Byrnes announced a "get tough" foreign policy toward the Soviet Union. The president ordered loyalty investigations of government employees. American Communist Party leaders were jailed.

The tide of anti-Communism kept growing in the West. In the United States "commies" and "pinks" (liberals) were harassed, and people were persecuted for their political opinions. Senator Joseph McCarthy stirred up the nation against liberals, Democrats, college teachers (whom he scornfully called "eggheads"), artists, and writers; in Congress the House Un-American Activities Committee searched out suspected Communists in Hollywood. Anti Communism became a test for patriotism and loyalty to Uncle Sam.

THE TRUMAN DOCTRINE AND THE MARSHALL PLAN

The Truman Doctrine, in 1947, was a reaction to Stalin's anti-Western policies. The United States reversed a nonintervention policy of 150 years and offered aid to Greece and Turkey and any country, however far away, that was threatened with Communism or pressure from the Soviet bloc.

Another U.S. move aroused Stalin's hostility. The U.S. secretary of state George C. Marshall created the European Recovery Program, the "Marshall Plan." It was a policy of enlightened self-interest: the United States wanted to help the war-torn nations of Europe to recover quickly, partly as a spur to international trade, but also as a protection against the spread of Soviet influence.

Through the Marshall Plan, the United States offered aid to all the war-wrecked countries of Europe. Czechoslovakia, Yugoslavia, and Poland voted to accept Marshall Plan aid, but they changed their minds under pressure from the Soviet government, for Stalin now felt himself ringed with hostile governments and U.S. military bases.

THE BERLIN AIRLIFT

In 1948 the Soviet government tested the opposing powers. Germany had been divided into zones of occupation after the war. The capital, Berlin, was also divided among the Big Three; but the city itself was deep within the Russian zone. Now Stalin threw up a blockade between East and West Germany, isolating Berlin. The Western sector of Berlin had no access to food, fuel, medical supplies, or any of the supplies of day-to-day life.

Stalin hoped that the West Berliners would have to join the Soviet sector or starve; and he thought the Western Allies would be frozen or starved out of the city altogether. He did not believe that the West would use armed force and risk starting another war just to keep West Berlin out of Russian hands. The United States and Britain met him with an answer that avoided military action and won the propaganda war.

The Berlin airlift was an advertisement for United States economic power (and the efficiency that Stalin always admired). And it showed British and American determination to scotch any Russian expansion. Each day, the United States and Britain flew more than 4,000 tons of supplies into Berlin, and incredibly they did it for almost a year, until Stalin finally lifted the blockade.

In the end Stalin's determination to wall off Russia and her satellites from the rest of the world produced an alliance against him. The North Atlantic Treaty Organization (NATO), a defense alliance of North American and European nations, came into being in 1949.

The Cold War lasted until Stalin's death, and well after, fed by the fears and ambitions of both sides. An arms race increased fears of attack. Huge military budgets were spent. The Soviets developed their own atomic bomb, and less than a year after the United States, the USSR had its own hydrogen bomb.

CHAPTER 15

A LIFE
AND A DEATH

Stalin's seventieth birthday was celebrated with the usual hysterical adulation, but his life had become quite gray and grim. Since the war he had enjoyed no home life, no "family hearth." His routine was as usual: he shuttled every day between the Kremlin and one of his *dachas*, or country houses. He was driven to the *dacha* in the evening, heavily guarded, over empty roads. He had dinner late and met there with the members of the Politburo (who had to drive out there after a long day at the Kremlin); he went to bed in the small hours of the morning, on a sofa in the room where he worked and spent his time. He slept late and was driven back to the Kremlin in the afternoon.

Politburo members came to Stalin's *dacha* without their wives and often had to sit through long dinners that began after midnight and lasted until early morning. They were encouraged to drink until they were sick, and to make fools of themselves playing juvenile practical jokes (salt in the vodka,

137

tomato on the chair,[1] guessing games with the penalty measured in glasses of vodka the loser had to toss back) while Stalin looked on.

A Yugoslav minister present at one of these dinners in 1948 was struck by the change in Stalin and the emptiness and loss of dignity of the old man and his "court." It was "both tragic and ugly," he says; there were the leaders of a great nation, "shut up in a narrow circle . . . inventing senseless reasons for drinking vodka."[2]

Stalin took no interest in his own eight grandchildren, although he took to decorating his wall with sentimental pictures of anonymous children, cut from magazines. He had loved his daughter as a child, calling her his little housekeeper, and teasing her gently. But now he rarely saw her. He became suspicious of her, and blamed her for marrying a Jew. His son Yakov was dead; his second wife, the idealistic Nadezhda, had killed herself in 1932; his other son, Vasily, was a boastful drunk whom Stalin seemed to despise.

The close-knit family group of the days before the war was gone—Stalin's wife and children, their aunts, uncles, grandparents, cousins, and friends. Now they were scattered. Most were dead; some had been shot, some jailed. His sisters-in-law, elderly widows, were imprisoned, one receiving a sentence of ten years' solitary confinement. They were "babblers," he said. They "knew too much" and "talked too much."

The only intimate portrait of Stalin's adult life comes from his daughter, Svetlana, who defected to the West in 1967. She calls him a "spiritual and moral monster," but she also paints a picture of a happy childhood, with a father who was happy, at least at home.[3] There were picnics in the woods, cooking pheasant eggs in hot ashes. There was the

Stalin holding twelve-year-old Svetlana.
She grew up to reject him, dropped the name
Stalin, and defected to the United States.

Stalin in 1920 with his second wife
Nadezhda, who committed suicide in 1932.

sunny *dacha* outside Moscow at Zubalovo, filled
with family and friends, where Bukharin, "whom
everyone adored," filled the house with tame animals—hedgehogs, a fox, and a hawk. Her father's
old friends were often there. Kirov was there, boat-
ing on the river.

But Bukharin, who had backed Stalin against
Trotsky, was dead, executed as a Trotskyite; Kirov
had been murdered; Stalin's old friends had committed suicide or were imprisoned or had been shot.
The *dacha* at Zubalovo was blown up as the Germans approached Moscow.

Now the aging despot was surrounded by toadies
and yes-men. His servants were NKVD people. His
food was tested for poison. The air in his *dacha* was
periodically sampled and tested. To make himself
secure he had ordered the purges; now he had no
one around but his terrified Politburo and the
NKVD. Stalin felt they would all get rid of him if
they could. He trusted no one. He was in the dusk,
surrounded by enemies, a shadow here, a movement
in the bushes there . . . Now the old tiger bared his
teeth for one last time.

THE DOCTORS' PLOT

In 1952 Moscow began to sense rumblings; the
country was given to understand that there were
more enemies than ever. As socialism advanced,
more vigilance would be required. Jewish spies,
working for the United States, were said to be hiding in every cupboard.

Members of the Politburo, which was now called
the Praesidium, sensed a change in Stalin's attitude
toward them. He would ask one or another, "Why
are your eyes so shifty today?" or "Why are you
avoiding looking me directly in the eyes?"4 Every-

one was nervous; it seemed obvious that Stalin was again suspicious of a "palace revolt" and was working up to another top-level purge.

They knew it would begin with the discovery of some conspiracy, but the conspiracy, when it was announced, was even more fantastic than usual. In January 1953, nine distinguished doctors who served in the Kremlin itself were accused as foreign agents conspiring to kill top government officials. Most of them were Jews, supposed to be working for the United States. They were tortured—Khrushchev says on Stalin's orders: "If you do not obtain confessions from the doctors," Stalin said to a security official, "we will shorten you by a head."[5]

The confessions would be used to implicate anyone else Stalin did not trust. Molotov, Malenkov, Beria—all the Praesidium were frightened.

No one knows just what Stalin planned, for in March, while he was alone in his locked room at his *dacha,* a blood vessel burst in his brain; he was partly paralyzed and unable to speak. Three days later, on March 5, he thrust up his arm in a sudden enigmatic gesture and died. He was seventy-three years old.

Most of the Kremlin doctors survived their ordeal; the impending purge was called off; and the members of government lived to carry on, except for Beria, head of the NKVD, who was shortly tried as a foreign agent and shot.

STALIN: THE ENIGMA

Who and what was Stalin? What motivated him? And how did he manage to hold a huge nation in such a grip of steel? His daughter, Svetlana, says: "He chose the way of a revolutionary because in him burned the cold flame of protest against society,

*Stalin lies in state. To the right are
Nikolai Bulganin and Nikita Khrushchev, who
later denounced Stalin for his "crimes."*

in which he himself was at the bottom of the ladder
and was supposed to remain there all his life."[6] She
comments sadly, "For twenty-seven years I was wit-
ness to the spiritual deterioration of my own father,
watching day after day how everything human in
him left him and how gradually he turned into a
grim monument to his own self."[7]

He remains mysterious. In his "secret speech" in
1956 Khrushchev called him "irrational and para-
noid." But in 1949 he called Stalin "Our dear father
and wise teacher," and he wept at Stalin's bedside
when he died. Trotsky, in the throes of wishful
thinking, described Stalin as "Russia's greatest me-
diocrity," but Trotsky was consumed with hatred
and contempt where his rival was concerned.

Throngs of Russians mourned and revered him; many colleagues respected him; his household staff loved him without reservation and cried like babies the morning he died. He was buried beside Lenin, and people were crushed to death in the crowds who came to bid him farewell.

In 1956 the Soviet government turned on Stalin and all his works. Khrushchev made his now famous "secret speech." He denounced Stalin and cleared the names of his victims. The speech would have caused havoc with the people, so it was not reported in the Soviet news. Copies were given to Party leaders to start the slow process of "de-Stalinization." Stalin's body was moved to an inconspicuous grave behind the Kremlin walls.

A biographer who wishes to be objective has a problem in writing about Stalin. The history of his years is so violent that reading contemporary accounts is like bathing in blood. Was there nothing good about Stalin? What did he accomplish?

A prominent Stalin biographer, Isaac Deutscher, once wrote this famous phrase about him. "He found Russia equipped with a wooden plow and left her equipped with atomic piles." It is true that under his regime a peasant nation became an industrial power. And, with the five-year plans, Stalin presided over the world's first attempt at a planned economy, imitated in one degree or another by many governments since. It is certainly true that he equipped Russia with hospitals and schools as well as bombs and tractors.

Deutscher concludes that to preserve this "better part of Stalin's work," history will have to sternly cleanse and reshape that work.[8] That is the task that later generations of Soviet leaders have slowly undertaken. That is the burden that Mikhail Gorbachev shouldered when he became the Soviet leader in 1985.

But Stalin solved "the peasant problem" with mass slaughter and in the course of it set Soviet agriculture back so far that Gorbachev and the other Soviet leaders are still struggling with its problems of depleted soil, unproductive farms, and inefficient organization. The bureaucracy that Stalin created has a life of its own and has proved almost impossible to dismantle; it became one of Mikhail Gorbachev's gravest problems when he succeeded to power and attempted to make Soviet society more open and stimulate its economy.

The more we learn as Soviet archives are opened and historical details revealed, the more fantastic we find Stalin's exercise of absolute power, and the more we are reminded of Lord Acton's famous phrase, "Power corrupts, and absolute power corrupts absolutely."

But the basic mechanism of power grew out of a one-party system that allowed no diversity of opinion, had no rules for orderly change, and employed an organization of secret police who were outside the law.

Once Stalin got a grip on the Party, there was no stopping him, but he changed Russia forever, and his impact on the modern world has been beyond measure.

CHRONOLOGY

Before January 31, 1918, the Russians followed the old-style (Julian) calendar. The new-style calendar, which we use today, was adopted in February 1918. The dates here all follow the new calendar.

1870	Birth of Lenin
1879	December 9, birth of Stalin
1894	Stalin enters Tiflis Theological Seminary.
1899	Stalin leaves seminary.
1904(?)	Stalin marries first wife, Ekaterina Svanidze.
1905	Bloody Sunday in St. Petersburg.
1908	Stalin's son Yakov is born. Stalin in prison or exile on and off most of the time until the Revolution.
1909	Death of Stalin's wife
1912	January. Lenin chooses Stalin, still in exile, as member of the Central Committee of the Bolshevik party.
1914	August; beginning of World War I

1917	March. Revolt against the czar (end of February, old style calendar, thus often called the February Revolution).
1917	March 15 (March 2, old style). Czar abdicates. Provisional government formed. Stalin arrives in Petrograd end of March.
1917	November 6–7 (October old style calendar, thus often called the October Revolution). Bolsheviks take over, arrest provisional government in Winter Palace. Stalin named commissar of nationalities in first Bolshevik government.
1918	Constituent Assembly meets, but is disbanded by Bolsheviks.
1918–1921	Civil War: "Reds" vs. "Whites"
1921	Famine
1922	April. Stalin becomes general secretary of the Central Committee of the Russian Communist party.
1924	Death of Lenin. Zinoviev, Kamenev, and Stalin rule.
1926	Stalin begins rise to one-man rule. Trotsky, Zinoviev, Kamenev all expelled from Politburo.
1929	Stalin's 50th birthday; beginning of his cult. First five-year plan. Stalin announces "liquidation of kulaks as a class." Purges begin.
1932–33	Famine
1936–1938	Three Moscow "show trials," and execution of Old Bolsheviks and Red Army officers.
1939	Nonaggression pact between Stalin and Hitler.
1939	September. German invasion of Poland. Beginning of World War II.
1941	June 22. Germany invades the Soviet Union.
1943	Teheran Conference of the "Big Three" (Roosevelt, Stalin, Churchill).

1945	February. Yalta Conference of the Big Three.
	September; end of World War II
1946	Beginning of the Cold War
1953	Beginning of the "doctors' plot"
1953	March 5; death of Stalin
1956	Khrushchev's "Secret Speech" on the crimes of Stalin.

SOURCE NOTES

CHAPTER 1: YOUNG STALIN, OLD RUSSIA

1. Leon Trotsky, *My Life* (New York: Grosset & Dunlap, 1930 and 1960), p. 480.
2. Edward Ellis Smith, *The Young Stalin* (New York: Farrar, Straus & Giroux, 1967), p. 34, and many sources.

CHAPTER 2: THE YOUNG REVOLUTIONARY

1. From a speech Stalin made in 1926, quoted in Bertram Wolfe, *Three Who Made a Revolution*, Vol. 2 (New York: Time Incorporated, 1964), p. 175.
2. Emil Ludwig, *Stalin* (New York: G. P. Putnam's Sons, 1942), p. 19. Also Smith, *The Young Stalin*, p. 35.
3. Isaac Deutscher, *Stalin: A Political Biography*, 2d ed. (New York: Oxford University Press paperback, 1967), p. 37.
4. Smith, *The Young Stalin*, p. 87.
5. *Ibid.*, p. 87 (quoting Iremashvili).
6. Seweryn Bialer, ed., *Stalin and His Generals: Soviet Military Memoirs of World War II* (Boulder: Westview

Press, a Westview Encore Reprint, 1984). Also in Khrushchev's "secret speech."
7. Smith, The Young Stalin, pp. 98–102 and chapters 3, 4, 5. Smith goes into great detail to advance the thesis that Stalin was a spy for the Okhrana early in his career.

CHAPTER 3: THE REVOLUTIONARIES

1. Alan Moorehead, The Russian Revolution (New York: Harper & Brothers, 1958), p. 82, quoting the Russian historian Pokrovsky.
2. A & Z, Lenin for Beginners (New York: Pantheon Books, 1978), p. 61, quoting Lenin in 1902.
3. Quoted in Wolfe, Three Who Made a Revolution, Vol. 1, p. 313.
4. David Killingray, The Russian Revolution (St. Paul, Minn.: Greenhaven Press, 1980), p. 22 (documents).
5. Ibid.
6. Wolfe, Three Who Made a Revolution, Vol. 1, p. 354.

CHAPTER 4: REVOLT AND WAR (1905–1917)

1. Wolfe, Three Who Made a Revolution, Vol. 2, p. 149.
2. Smith, The Young Stalin, p. 291.
3. Svetlana Alliluyeva, Only One Year (New York: Harper & Row, 1969), p. 381.
4. Quoted in Montgomery H. Hyde, Stalin: The History of a Dictator (New York: Farrar, Straus and Giroux, 1971), p. 91, also many other sources.

CHAPTER 5: THE BOLSHEVIK REVOLUTION (1917)

1. From Winston Churchill, The World Crisis, cited in Moorehead, The Russian Revolution, p. 173.
2. Trotsky, My Life, p. 333.
3. N. Sukhanov, Notes of the Revolution, quoted in Leon Trotsky, The Russian Revolution (New York: Doubleday & Company, 1959), p. 216, and Moorehead, The Russian Revolution, pp. 166–167.
4. John Reed, Ten Days that Shook the World (New York: The Modern Library, 1935), p. 126.

5. "I. V. Djugashvili" for Iosif Vissarion, etc. Iosif is a form of Joseph.

CHAPTER 6: ONE PARTY RULES THE STATE

1. Moorehead, *The Russian Revolution*, pp. 268–269.
2. Stalin, quoted in Joel Carmichael, *Stalin's Masterpiece* (New York: St. Martin's Press, 1976), p. 11.
3. Quoted in Irving Werstein, *Ten Days in November* (Philadelphia: Macrae Smith Company, 1967), p. 101.

CHAPTER 7: STALIN HOLDS ON

1. Quoted in Moshe Lewin, *Lenin's Last Struggle* (New York: Random House, 1968), p. 152, and many other sources.
2. Quoted in many sources, inclg. Nikita Khrushchev, *Krushchev Speaks* (Ann Arbor: University of Michigan Press, 1963), p. 210.
3. *Ibid.*
4. Lewin, *Lenin's Last Struggle*, pp. 77–84.
5. Mikhail Heller and Aleksandr M. Nekrich, *Utopia in Power* (New York: Summit Books, 1986), p. 207.

CHAPTER 8: HISTORY REVISED

1. From an address given by Stalin in 1913. Quoted in Wolfe, *Three Who Made a Revolution*, Vol. 2, p. 142, also many other sources.
2. *Ibid.*, Vol. 2, p. 131ff. Also in Khrushchev's "secret speech."

CHAPTER 9: THE WAR AGAINST THE PEASANTS

1. Heller and Nekrich, *Utopia in Power*, p. 117.
2. Quoted from Stalin's works in Heller and Nekrich, *Utopia in Power*, p. 233.
3. Stephen F. Cohen, *Bukharin and the Bolshevik Revolution* (New York: Oxford University Press, 1980), pp. 176–177, and many sources.

4. Heller and Nekrich, *Utopia in Power*, p. 233.
5. *Ibid.*, and many other sources.
6. John Bartlett, *Familiar Quotations*, 14th ed. (Boston: Little, Brown and Company, 1968), p. 954.
7. Hyde, *Stalin: The History of a Dictator*, p. 380.
8. Quoted in many sources, with slight differences in translation: "we do it or we go under"; "we do it or they crush us"; "we will be crushed," etc.
9. Winston Churchill, *The Hinge of Fate* (Boston: Houghton Mifflin Company, 1950), p. 499.
10. Mark Levene, *Arthur Koestler* (New York: Frederick Ungar), p. 12.

CHAPTER 10: THE WAY THINGS WERE

1. Andrew Smith, *I Was a Soviet Worker* (New York: E. P. Dutton & Co., 1936), p. 181.
2. W. G. Krivitsky, *I Was Stalin's Agent* (London: The Right Book Club, 1940), p. 10.
3. H. G. Wells, *Experiment in Autobiography* (New York: J. B. Lippincott Company, 1967), p. 689.
4. Lincoln Steffens, *The Letters of Lincoln Steffens*, Vol. I (New York: Harcourt, Brace and Company, 1938), p. 463.
5. Alliluyeva, *Only One Year*, p. 387.
6. Yevgeny Yevtushenko, *A Precocious Autobiography* (New York: E. P. Dutton & Company, 1963), pp. 67–68.
7. Khrushchev, *Khrushchev Speaks*, p. 253.
8. Alliluyeva, *Only One Year*, p. 369.
9. Khrushchev, *Khrushchev Speaks*, p. 213.
10. "Big Brother," the name applied to the all-powerful and pervasive dictator in George Orwell's novel, *1984*.
11. Heller and Nekrich, *Utopia in Power*: 1932, theft of state property (e.g. tools) warranted death penalty; 1934, death penalty made only punishment for betrayal of the fatherland; 1935, all criminal penalties including capital punishment extended to children 12 or older, p. 739.

CHAPTER 11: THE GREAT TERROR

1. Alliluyeva, *Twenty Letters to a Friend*, p. 114.
2. Trotsky, *My Life*, p. 450.
3. Boris Souvarine, *Stalin: A Critical Survey of Bolshevism* (New York: Octagon Books, 1972), p. 485, and many sources.
4. Khrushchev, *Khrushchev Speaks*, p. 261.
5. *Ibid.*, p. 233.
6. Joseph E. Davies, *Mission to Moscow* (New York: Simon and Schuster, 1941), pp. 43–45.
7. Krivitsky, *I Was Stalin's Agent*. This is Krivitsky's conviction, having been in the Soviet secret service and followed the events. It is discussed in detail in his book.

CHAPTER 12: STALIN AND HITLER

1. Quoted in Hyde, *Stalin: The History of a Dictator*, p. 464.

CHAPTER 13: WORLD WAR II

1. Nikita Khrushchev, *Khrushchev Remembers: The Last Testament* (Boston: Little, Brown and Company, 1974), p. 169.
2. Hyde, *Stalin: The History of a Dictator*, pp. 438–439.
3. Deutscher, *Stalin: A Political Biography* (New York: Oxford University Press paperback, 1967), p. 463.
4. Churchill, *The Hinge of Fate*, p. 482.
5. Alliluyeva, *Only One Year*, p. 370.
6. Harrison Salisbury, *The 900 Days: The Siege of Leningrad* (New York: Harper & Row, 1969), part IV.
7. Churchill, *The Hinge of Fate*, p. 201.
8. Deutscher, *Stalin: A Political Biography*, p. 505.
9. Heller and Nekrich, *Utopia in Power*, p. 443.

CHAPTER 14: THE COLD WAR

1. Winston Churchill, *Address*, Westminster College, Fulton, Missouri, March 5, 1946.

CHAPTER 15: A LIFE AND A DEATH

1. Alliluyeva, *Only One Year*, p. 385.
2. Milovan Djilas, *Conversations With Stalin* (New York: Harcourt, Brace & World, 1962), pp. 151–152.
3. Alliluyeva, *Twenty Letters to a Friend*, throughout, particularly chapter 3.
4. Khrushchev, *Khrushchev Speaks*, p. 232.
5. *Ibid.*, p. 248.
6. Alliluyeva, *Only One Year*, p. 362.
7. *Ibid.*, p. 142.
8. Deutscher, *Stalin: A Political Biography*, p. 628.

FURTHER READING

These are a few books with a clear and forthright style that should make them of interest to young readers. See the source notes for further titles, most of which are not included here for reasons of space.

Alliluyeva, Svetlana. *Only One Year.* New York: Harper and Row, 1969.

————. *Twenty Letters to a Friend.* New York: Harper and Row, 1967. (Intimate glimpses of Stalin by his daughter.)

Andreyev, Olga Chernov. *Cold Spring in Russia.* Ann Arbor, MI: Ardis, 1978.

Begin, Menachem. *White Nights: The Story of a Prisoner in Russia.* 1957. Reprint. New York: Harper and Row, 1977. (This is a vivid account of the former Israeli prime minister's experience in the Soviet labor camps.)

Khrushchev, Nikita. *Khrushchev Remembers.* Edited by Strobe Talbott. Boston: Little, Brown and Company, 1970. (This amounts to an oral history, informal and fascinating.)

Snow, C. P. *Variety of Men.* New York: Charles Scribner's Sons, 1967.

Solzhenitsyn, Aleksandr. *One Day in the Life of Ivan Denisovich.* New York: New American Library, 1963.
Trotsky, Leon. *Portraits, Political and Personal.* New York: Pathfinder Press, 1977.
Yevtushenko, Yevgeny. *A Precocious Autobiography.* New York: E. P. Dutton and Co., 1963.

INDEX